Child of Light

Teresa Koska

Child of Light

Teresa Koska

Book Written By: Teresa Koska
Cover Art By: Teresa Koska
Illustrations by: Teresa Koska
https://fineartamerica.com/art/teresa+koska

Distributed by:
Atlanta's ART, LLC
AtlantasART.com

Cover Design by: Atlanta Marie Carrera

© 2023 Atlanta Marie Carrera

Published by:
Heir Media Publishing
5041 New Centre Drive, Suite 123
Wilmington, NC USA

A CIP record for this book is available from the Library of Congress Cataloging-in-Publication Data
ISBN-13: 979-8-9859254-2-5
Printed in USA

Contents

A Message from Teresa's Sister

As I drove to the Hospice center to be with my younger sister, Teresa, I was numb. It was just so hard to believe that I was losing her to breast cancer. There was nothing left to even say. Tears streaming down my face, I just kept thinking how the world was soon going to be without this beautiful spirit, this wonderfully uplifting soul that has graced us all for the past 47 years.

Just as these thoughts entered my brain, I saw before me the most amazing sunset... spreading light... full of miraculous colors as far as the eye could see. I knew that as an artist, Teresa would appreciate the extra effort God put into that sunset – her last one.

That's the moment these words came into my head... "Child of Light." I kept repeating the unfolding poem, over and over again, so that I wouldn't miss one word until I could write it down. As soon as I arrived at my destination, I sat in the parking lot and scribbled down the poem. Then, I walked in to hold my sister's hand.

I know God gave me those words, just like He gave Teresa the words you are about to hear from her emails and blog. What I didn't know then was that this would be the title we use for her book, "Child of Light" – and yes, she was, in every sense of the word!

— Atlanta Marie Carrera (Teresa's Sister)

Child of Light

A child of light,
slipping into the setting sun.

A brilliance of white,
transforming darkness into life.

A spirit of love,
joining us all in prayer as one.

A freedom above,
Celebrating in unending joy.

Poem by Atlanta Marie Carrera

My Promises...

Teresa knew she was running out of time to publish her faith-filled journey that she wanted to share with as many people as possible. She was holding onto this world as long as she could and wrote as much as she could in that final year.

I made my sister a promise that I would do whatever I could to see her dream realized. This book is that promise in progress. I send it out into the world in the way she wanted — not as her story to be told, but for God's glory to be seen.

Teresa's further wish was to give back to charity. The Special Olympics was near and dear to her heart, and so, a portion of the proceeds from this book and Teresa's art will be donated to the Special Olympics of North Carolina in her memory.

And finally, all additional proceeds from this book and from Teresa's art will be given to her son. I thank you all for helping me fulfill my promise.

— *Atlanta Marie Carrera* (Teresa's Sister)

Dedication

Teresa wanted to thank God
for carrying her through her journey.

She also wanted to thank her family, friends, and
neighbors for being so supportive over the years.

She had a special thank you for
Dr. Kelly Marcom at Duke Cancer Center
— may he find a cure.

Most importantly,
Teresa expressed her greatest joy
in her son,
to whom she dedicated this book.

Foreword

In TK's Words...

This book was written especially for you or someone you know who is struggling. God is good, and He is not surprised by what life has in store for you. He is prepared to walk you through any hardship... all you have to do is accept His gift of perseverance, as He turns curses into blessings.

During my cancer journey, I struggled with day-to-day problems — divorce, financial ruin, catching up, broken things, etc. Through it all, God reminded me that He gave me a gift, and I needed to share it with you. He wanted you to have it. That is why it is in your hands now.

I almost let personal insecurity stop me from sharing my story. I'm not a famous author; I'm just like you... a regular person. It's a true story about my life getting turned upside down and inside out in the quickest moments.

I went into survival mode, and then, something miraculous happened. I took a rollercoaster ride and learned more about myself through cancer than others learn in a lifetime.

What I didn't expect was the outpouring of how sharing my personal journey through a blog has helped everyone I knew with their own problems, and the ripple effect was huge.

Selfishly, I thought that this was my life and my story only. It took me a long time to figure out that God intended for me to share my learning experience with you, so you could grow.

I pray that you find something in my words, God's words, to help you move past the bitterness of the negative things that invade your life. You can move forward; do more; become more.

There is no doubt in my mind that you can rise above your circumstances. I know this to be true: God keeps His promises.

One of my favorite verses in the Bible: "I can do all things through Christ who strengthens me." (Philippians 4:13). It may not always be easy, and sometimes it's downright almost unbearable... but the valleys don't last forever.

God wants us to enjoy many gifts, but we have to be willing to uncover our eyes and open our hearts to see His blessings in disguise.

Your sister in Christ,

Teresa "TK"

My Letter to all Cancer Patients

I'm sorry you have cancer...and not the "better you than me" kind of sorry, but the "you don't deserve to be sick" kind of sorry. I know nobody understands what you're going through and the fear that is your constant companion. I know you are suffering beyond any sickness you've ever known. I know there are no easy answers or quick fixes.

I'm sorry your life revolves around your treatment schedule and your medications. I'm sorry you are tired of getting pricked by needles and undergoing scans, tests, chemo or surgery. I'm sorry that you cry sometimes and feel a sense of loss over the life you used to have before cancer. I'm sorry that you have so many "bad" days. I'm sorry you have to watch your family cry.

I truly wish there was a cure for you that would last forever – a cure with no side effects or pain; a cure that didn't cost a fortune, only available to a certain few. I truly wish I could wave a magic wand and replace every hard moment you are going through with a happy memory instead.

All I can do is tell you that you are amazing! You really are. I have the deepest respect for you. I don't know anybody tougher than a cancer patient.

Any person that makes the sacrifices you make to be here for the ones you love should get fireworks every night. I don't have to know you to pray for you and for a cure. Take care of yourself and know that you are not alone.

Sincerely Yours,

Teresa

Chapter 1

One Year

"Therefore we do not lose heart. Though outwardly we are wasting away, yet inwardly we are being renewed day by day. For our light and momentary troubles are achieving for us an eternal glory that far outweighs them all. So we fix our eyes not on what is seen, but on what is unseen, since what is seen is temporary, but what is unseen is eternal."

— 2 Corinthians 4:16-18

Last night, I was thinking about the memories I will make this year. How will I pack in everything I want to do? How will I make each day count? How will I get my son to be "present" in the moment and not dwell on the whens and what ifs about my health (me too for that matter)?

Within each month, two weeks are automatically taken away from me by medical appointments and recovery periods. Each day that passes, I'm painfully aware that I might not see this month on my calendar ever again.

As I thought about these things, I grabbed my Bible and asked God, "What do you say about this worry that has my attention?" I just opened up my Bible and these were the exact words that my eyes fell to on the page:

"You will give me added years of life, as rich and full as those of many generations, all packed into one. And I shall live

before The Lord forever. Oh send your loving kindness and truth to guard and watch over me, and I will praise your name continually, fulfilling my vow of praising you each day."

— Psalm 61:6-8

Wow! He never lets me down. Not ever. When you seek His wisdom, everything falls into place so much easier. Words are encouraging, but belief makes them real. I'm not speaking flowery, hopeful words here – I mean it. It's nice to walk in confidence. It's nice to have someone that constantly keeps their promises to me. My life is not what I thought it would be, but at least I know I can depend on an unfailing love that surpasses what I deserve.

I know that I will enjoy an amazing eternal life after this earthly one, and God will hold my hand this year until I can go home. After I leave, I can be confident that He will hold the hands of all my loved ones with each passing day, month, and year. One true God. My one true love. My one year to make each day count like they never have before with my friends and family.

My Prayer

Thank You God for being ever present in my life. Thank You for not leaving me empty. Thank You for comforting me during my times of trouble. Most of all Thank You for preparing a place for me to be with You forever. I know I can depend on You for all my needs. I'm so glad You are on the throne.

Amen.

The Physical and Spiritual Fight

As I lay in bed, helpless to stop what's in front of me, I'm thinking of the list of side effects I will have to tackle one by one over the next few days, mostly on my own.

The shaking hands, the all-over fevers, the sweating, the pain in my mouth and jaw, the stomach, leg and foot cramping, the indigestion, the hunger, the sleep deprivation from steroids, the remainder of my hair falling out and the hair follicle pain that makes it difficult to lay my head on a pillow, the blurry vision, the burning stomach pain from a shot on Friday, the dry itchy skin, the rashes on my face and feet, the nerve pain in my hands and feet that make every day activities (like writing or walking) difficult, the constant nausea, the joint pain, the bulging discs and massive cancer on my spine that makes me cry and endure indescribable back pain.

It truly makes me realize how awful Hell must be...the constant unending torture.

I will at least get some relief in five days.

That's a brief list of my physical struggles. It's hard to believe that my spiritual struggles are actually harder. The biggest item on my spiritual struggle list is to forgive those who have done cruel things to me.

The lies, empty promises, disappointments, complete abandonment, and exclusion. It's a challenge to look at people through the eyes of Jesus: to forgive, no matter what. To give second, third, fourth, and fifth chances. To extend love knowing I might never receive it in return from some. To start each new day with a clean slate. You see, pain runs so deep that it scars the bone (and I have the scans to prove it).

I must overlook offenses in order to heal.

If left to myself, I would harbor anger, bitter resentment, jealousy, self pity and want to seek justice... but I'm not leaving it to myself to fix the unfixable. I'm going to God's word and building my spiritual faith.

I need your help too. A prayer is the most powerful tool you have to fix the unfixable for me and for yourself. I desperately need your help in my physical and spiritual fight. I've listed every problem I could think of at this moment. Please look at this list and pick something specific to pray for me.

One burden at a time, I'm going to work on lifting them away from me until I have total healing.

Thank you for not giving up on me. I don't want to roll over and wait to die. I want the world to see the mighty power of God! Let it begin with me...let it begin with God's mercy.

Passing the Test

As I go on my downward spiral, I realized that this all might just be a test:

I will pass, fail, or succeed with flying colors. God is using my circumstances to teach me...to teach others...to toughen me up. My road has not been easy. I cry thinking, "I just can't take this anymore." Every day brings a new challenge that I just don't want. I've never known such constant pain and suffering.

I believe there are no coincidences. Every single detail of my life is there for a very specific reason. God allows things to happen in our lives to refine us. Our "uncomfortable" situations are our tests.

He is trying to grow our strength, patience, trust, and faith. He is testing our optimism, loyalty, and unselfishness. I've had to let go of my vanity, pride, security, independence, and freedom throughout my cancer process.

God is trying to make us better through our adversity. He is in complete control. Fighting against God is fruitless. Until we learn acceptance and relinquish our own control, we will never be open to His teachable moments. The greatest thing that I have learned is to have FAITH and TRUST in God— not only regardless of my circumstances but especially during my most difficult circumstances.

You see, God is constant: He never changes. We are the ones that change and grow and learn. All I care about is God being pleased with me and how I handled my adversity. Many people remain bewildered and even mad at God for how I'm being tortured on a daily basis (I even told my son, "If I died tomorrow, don't you dare be mad at God...neither one of us would be here in the first place if not for Him.").

For the record, I love God just as much if not more today than I did during my happiest lifetime moments. I know He loves me. I know He sacrificed His only Son for me. I know that in the end, I will be rewarded for my Faith. Those are all good things.

Pray that I will pass this test. Pray that self defeating thoughts would flee from my mind. Pray that God will reward my faith with compassion. Pray that I will learn and teach quickly. Pray that nothing I endure will ever be in vain. Pray that God will swiftly turn everything meant for my harm into something good.

I WILL pass this test. I will have faith and trust in God's plans for me. I will love The Lord with all my heart every single day. He is preparing me for His glory, and I gladly accept His will for my life.

Fear Not

"Fear not, for I am with you; Be not dismayed, FOR I AM YOUR GOD. I will strengthen you, Yes, I will help you, I will uphold you with my righteous right hand."

— Isaiah 41:10

I didn't realize how many times God says "Fear not," or "Don't be afraid" in the Bible; He said it hundreds of times, but who's keeping count. He knew we would need that reassurance over and over and over again.

I don't know about you, but I'm afraid. I'm afraid the pain I'm in will never let me go. I'm afraid that when I die, my son will be devastated. I'm afraid of needles. I'm afraid of forgetting to take one of my pills.

I'm afraid of not being able to pay for everything. I'm afraid that I will never have a romantic love interest. I'm afraid I will never have eyebrows, eyelashes, or hair ever again. I'm afraid I will never lose all the weight I've gained from the steroids I'm on. I'm afraid I won't find clothes to fit me this winter. I'm afraid that every time I go out in public, people stare at me and it will make me uncomfortable. I'm afraid I will feel unattractive until the day I die.

I'm afraid I will never get "caught up" so I can relax. I'm afraid I will miss all the milestones of my son's life. I'm afraid of germs and getting sick. I'm afraid I will never have energy for a whole day ever again. I'm afraid that my last months on earth will be unbearable. I'm afraid of many things.

And when I cry or pray or plead with God, He says "Do Not Be Afraid." How can I not be afraid when all these worries and stresses are on my doorstep? Because God is with me. God is with you. God Helps and Strengthens all of us.

Yes, the things we fear are real things, but so is God...and God is BIGGER than our fears. He's more powerful. God is NEVER afraid of anything because everything is under His control. I wouldn't be afraid if I was Him either, and that's the whole point. We are not alone. God is with us.

We should not be afraid of what the world dishes out, because God has the ability to make fear disappear. God instills confidence and a conqueror's attitude. Nothing is beyond God's reach or command.

I've seen the mighty power of God in action. It's like watching a hurricane or tornado rip through and destroy anything in its path. God can do that with our fear. He can destroy it. He can obliterate it. He can crush fear into little itty bitty too small to recognize pieces. Fear will come and go, in and out of our thoughts, but God is our constant.

God doesn't leave. God will repeat this message to us as many times as we need to hear it: "FEAR NOT, FOR I AM WITH YOU."

You Go God! Thanks for having me covered. Take my weakness and replace it with your strength. I'm so glad I'm yours.

Remember Where You Are... Earth

We are so wrapped up in the day to day comings and goings that it's easy to let our eyes rest upon the here and now. We are living in the world...on earth...and as Christians, BELOW our home! Things here are poor and unsatisfying.

For me, life on earth has been a daily physical torture. I'm reminded constantly that Satan wants to attack me while he still has a chance to touch me. I keep telling myself that, "This too shall pass."

God is jealous when we set our hearts on the attractions of the earth. We get so easily distracted from Him. I read somewhere that, "Earth is just a stage erected as our passage to the place Jesus has gone to prepare for us." The Earth as we know it, in all its false attractions, will dwindle and pass away. It will suffer its own death before its rebirth eventually. The world is putting on a show and sometimes, if we're not careful, we get stuck looking at the show. Satan succeeds in those moments.

We need to look beyond...look above...look to Jesus who has an outstretched hand to lead us away from this place. Your home isn't here. Your home is in God's closeness. It's a beautiful place that exudes everything good.

Going through my sickness lifted a final veil for me. I could see earth and heaven much more clearly.

How ugly the earth has become to me. It makes me want to build a protective nest from the stings of men's arrows and the temptations of excess the earth has to offer.

I look around and wonder, "Do others see what I see?"... The entitlement, selfishness, laziness, and total lack of gratitude? How did that happen? How many wrong turns and bad decisions have to happen in our lives in order for us to see where we are exactly on our path to Heaven?

It should be a straight shot. Simple. Easy. I'm here; I want to be there. It should be our ultimate goal. God does everything with purpose. If we are still on this earth, there is a very good reason. We have been shown the light and the truth. We want to rest in that light.

For now, while we are waiting for Jesus to say, "It's your time. Come Home," we have a job to do….a purpose to serve…a soul to save…and a God to glorify.

Being saved is not enough. If it were, I would buy you a bunch of calendars and you can just mark off your remaining days. Even from my sick bed, my role is to love others and serve God. I pray for every one of you out of love and hope that your eyes stay focused and your hearts face the right direction.

Heaven is where we will worship God forever. You might ask yourself what the difference is if you worship God every day here? To that, I would say that Heaven will not have earthly distractions and temptations. Heaven will be filled with souls that are of one mind and one thought and one love above all else.

> *"The Lord will rescue me from every evil attack and will bring me safely to his heavenly kingdom. To Him be glory for ever and ever. Amen."*
> — 2 Timothy 4:18

> *"You can enter God's Kingdom only through the narrow gate. The highway to hell is broad and it's gate is wide for the many who choose that way."*
> — Matthew 7:13

To the Point

"We are saved by trusting. And trusting means looking forward to getting something we don't yet have— for a man who already has something doesn't need to hope and trust that he will get it. But if we must keep trusting God for something that hasn't happened yet, it teaches us to wait patiently and confidently. And in the same way— by our faith— the Holy Spirit helps us with our daily problems and in our praying. For we don't even know what we should pray for, nor how to pray as we should; but the Holy Spirit prays for us with such feeling that it cannot be expressed in words. And the Father who knows all hearts knows, of course, what the Spirit is saying, as He pleads for us in harmony with God's own will. And we know that all that happens to us is working for our good if we love God and are fitting into his plans."

— Romans 8:24–28

I hope this verse grabs your heart and soul the way it did mine. I'm so happy to be HIS child.

After reading that passage, my problems just grew smaller and my CONFIDENCE, TRUST, and LOVE, can hardly be contained!!!.... to be so cared about is a comfort that has no boundaries. God bless you all!

23

Chapter 2

Glimpses of Light

Music, Poetry, and Art

"Instead of wondering when your next vacation is, maybe you should set up a life you don't need to escape from."
— Seth Godin

"A person should hear a little music, read a little poetry, and see a fine picture every day of their life, in order that worldly cares may not obliterate the sense of beauty which God has implanted in the human soul."
— Johann Wolfgang Von Goethe

Music, poetry, and art were the highlights of the Renaissance period. Contrary to that, we are currently living in the age of technology, meant to save time and be more efficient. Unfortunately, technology really seems to separate personal human contact, and it definitely does not feed our souls.

Am I crazy, or does it seem like we have less time than ever before? Have we fooled ourselves into thinking we can accomplish more, because of technology, so we pile our commitments on pretty thick? Thus, do we feel stressed and like we are failures if we can't do it all?

Music

Poetry

Art

I'm not sure about you, but that sounds way more appealing than answering texts, emails, etc. I'm going to try to incorporate those beautiful things into my life every day. I'm quite certain that it will help crowd out worldly nuisances and grow my appreciation for the great gifts of God.

Calm....here I come!!!

Dazzling Splendor

When was the last time you sat under a tree and marveled at its splendor?

I ate breakfast this morning on the back porch and studied every branch of a crepe myrtle tree that wraps its branches around my house, as if to protect it. Its limbs are impressive. They are graceful like the arms of a ballerina. Its leaves play music and dance when the wind comes strolling by. Its trunk grows so thick and strong that it has to shed its own bark to make room for its ever growing size. It is covered in blooms that are so big, it makes the branches lean toward the ground from the weight of the flowers and berries. If that's not splendor, I don't know what is.

"Lord, I love your home, this shrine where the brilliant, dazzling splendor of your presence lives."

— Psalm 26:8

He is here with us, you know. Look around at His splendor. He's given us countless things to marvel at...just for our enjoyment and proof of His presence.

Sit. Listen. Look. Touch. Smell. Taste. Don't miss another opportunity to spend time admiring the dazzling splendor of God. I'm rich in His gifts all around me. Isn't it time you received some of His gifts too? They are waiting on you; you are not waiting on them.

My Prayer

Father... Dad... I'm blown away by Your creation. I'm sorry that I often overlook the subtleties of Your gifts. Sometimes, You offer things with thunder and lightning, and sometimes, Your whisper is quieter than butterflies. I'm going to try harder to be still and use all my senses to admire the dazzling splendor You have created.

I don't say it enough... THANK YOU for being a constant giver of gifts. Thank You for surrounding me with your presence. I pray for better awareness instead of the numbness that noise creates in my life. YOU AMAZE ME!

I love You the way grass loves the rain.

Amen.

The Rain

I have never met anyone who loves the rain more than my son. He says it's so relaxing and soothing. When he has a bad day and it's raining, he thanks God for sending him comfort through the rain.

As an event planner, I always considered the rain an enemy, so to speak, preventing the perfect wedding. It will mess up the bride's hair. Now, we need tents and umbrellas. How's it going to look in pictures? I don't want to get spots on all my perfectly clean glass candle holders. It's going to cause delays. Everyone's shoes will get ruined. Trust me...I can make a really long list.

However, my son has recently converted me to liking it too. The grass gets greener. The flowers breathe a sigh of relief. We huddle up at home instead of going out. It's the closest sound to the hush of ocean waves. If you sit down and stay still for a little while, you can watch and listen to its rhythmic cascade. It's as beautiful as snow. It washes away dirt and dust and pollen: my son is highly allergic to pollen and dust.

If we women didn't care so much about a good hair day, it would actually feel good to feel the rain on your face...kind of like when you were a kid and ran through the sprinklers.

One of the things that stuck with me the most on all my many trips to Duke was the rain and the rainbows that came with it. It rained every single time I drove there in the first few weeks, without fail. "How dismal," I thought to myself. AND THEN, God would show me the most spectacular rainbows I've ever seen (including two double rainbows). It was my first sign of hope. A rainbow is God's promise to never flood the earth again. I felt like it was His promise to me that cancer was not going to drown me. During that time, I saw seven rainbows meaning seven promises, and God always kept His promise time after time. As I sat inside for many months, recovering, I was happy when it rained because it meant more people would come and visit me (everyone was busy when it was sunny). I also wasn't missing out on anything outside on rainy days, and I hate missing out.

Today, we celebrate my son's birthday. As I look outside and see a gray sky with rain coming down, I think, "My son will be so happy when he wakes up today because God remembered his favorite gift." As I get ready to get my first bone infusion, I will say the rain is helping me to stay calm. Mainly because now I see his excited smiling face when it rains, and that will always comfort me.

I hope you will find joy in the rain today too. The biggest lesson I have learned in life so far is that happiness is all about perspective not circumstances.

So...let it rain!

The World Needs More Crickets

Last night was one of those perfect weather evenings, not too hot and not too cold, but perfect enough to wrap yourself in a soft cuddly blanket on the back porch. The sky was draped in pitch black. The only light that pierced the darkness, in my backyard, was the up lighting on all of my trees and the dancing glow of flickering candlelight, against the porch railings, from the lanterns I had put out.

My son and I sat in the two chairs, snuggled up in blankets, on our back porch, and marveled at the peacefulness this evening brought. Shhh....listen. Crickets.... All in unison.... playing their own violins for our evening concert.

I thought to myself, "When God made crickets, did He plan on them gathering around our homes so many years later to sing a song of peacefulness?"

This night is why I fight to live another day for my son. All the needles, all the crying, all the long car rides, all the doctor's appointments, all the chemo rounds, all the blood work, all the scans, all the pills, all the pain, all the nausea, all the relentless suffering just for one night of sitting on the back porch with my son for four hours listening to the crickets and talking.

And you know what? IT WAS WORTH IT! I would do it all again to feel that closeness, love, and peace.

Our weary world needs a cricket night desperately. I can't take away hurts and problems from the ones I love. I wish I could. I really do. It hurts my heart to see them in emotional pain. But, I can say, "STOP what you're doing. STOP fixating on the never ending rushing river of problems that will be glad to drown you in the undertow. STOP listening to hurtful words and START listening to the crickets outside, who are trying to keep you calm with their music."

I know more than anyone about hurt... about pain... about problems... about suffering. I have had enough to last me 10 life times. I'm not going to let the weary world grab my hand and pull me under to be miserable with them. I know misery loves company. I'm shutting the door behind me to the porch.

As my mom said when I was little about shutting doors to the house, "MAKE UP YOUR MIND. YOU'RE EITHER IN OR YOU'RE OUT... DECIDE, AND SHUT THE DOOR."

Just me and my son on the back porch listening to crickets with the door shut behind us... as I breathed in the evening air all I could think about was,

"The world needs more crickets."

"The heavens declare the glory of God; the skies proclaim the work of His hands."
— Psalm 19:1

A Prayer for Joy in my Life

Please God,

Take this cloud of darkness away.

Shine Your light upon me.

Send Your angels to help me.

Give me the courage and strength

To start to feel the joy in my life again.

Amen

Chapter 3

Father of Light

How Great Are His Gifts

"NO EYE HAS SEEN, NO EAR HAS HEARD, AND NO MIND HAS IMAGINED what God has prepared for those who love Him."
— 1 Corinthians 2:9

Every day when we leave the house, I put a note on the door that my son and I read together, and it has changed our entire mindset for the better.

It reads: "We have the FAVOR of God today! Our problems are small because we serve a BIG God!"

"Praise The Lord, my soul, And forget not all His benefits — Who forgives all your sins and heals all your diseases, Who redeems your life from the pit and crowns you with love and compassion, Who satisfies your desires with good things So that your youth is renewed like the eagle's."
— Psalm 103:1-5

Who could ask for more than that? Forgiveness, Healing, Rescue, Love, Compassion, Satisfaction, and Renewed Youth.... all Great Gifts from above. Not everyone knows that these gifts are free to us and within our reach (just because we are His). Pretty awesome if you ask me! If you are a Christian, rejoice that you are blessed with these gifts. Praise The Lord for all of these benefits.

Pray for those who don't know Him. Pray for those who ignore Him. Pray for those who think that this short life on earth is all there is. Pray for all of them to see clearly that Jesus loves them beyond any love they have ever known.

How great are His gifts... How great is our Savior... Worthy to be praised forever!

(I'm especially looking forward to the "healing our diseases" part... I'm keeping the faith).

Nothing is too Hard for God!

"O Lord God! You have made the heavens and earth by your great power; Nothing is too hard for you!"

— Jeremiah 32:17

I'm just gonna lay it out here this morning and say that we act like stuff we have going on is too hard for God to fix....and by "we," I mean "me" for sure. I know that's true because occasionally little things creep into my thoughts by the name of: doubt, fear, anxiety, and worry. Ever have any of those thoughts.... Ever? Then welcome to my club where a whole nation is a member.

It's in the moments where I REMEMBER how God has stepped into my past, that I regain my confidence and hold on tight to my trust. If you look back at your life, you have to admit some things got fixed that you had nothing to do with. Then there are those skeptics who question...how do you know it's God and not fate, luck, or coincidence?

I can only speak from personal experience when I say, I would read a promise in the Bible, and then it would manifest itself in my life almost immediately. I would have a landslide of coincidences that would be impossible to ignore. An example of that would be a need fulfilled on the exact day I needed it to in the exact measure I needed. That "coincidence" would happen to me on a routine basis. I would beat all odds when it came to recovery from horrible accidents or illnesses. Lastly, I was witness to miracles. Things that I've seen, heard, and felt with my senses that were undeniably not explained by science (or ghosts for that matter).

If you haven't had any of those things happen to you, I would ask one simple question. How much time have you spent seeking God's love, will, and purpose for your life, and how much faith did you give God without "proof" of His existence? I'm not saying God manifests Himself the same way for all people. I am saying that if you seek God in earnest, you will find Him.

I don't care what problem you have on the table this morning; it is not too much for God to handle. My table is about to break because it's got so much stuff on it! Just when I hear a creak like it's going to collapse under the weight of my cancer as the last straw, I will have one burden lifted after another to lighten the load. Sometimes those burdens are lifted by friends, family, or strangers, and sometimes burdens are lifted by God Himself with regards to my body and spirit.

I will praise God until I take my last breath because He not only created me...He saved me. He saved me from myself and bad choices, He saved me from sin and death (repeatedly) and He saved me from a meaningless, empty life. With Him, I am complete.

I can have stage 4 cancer and be the happiest, most optimistic, and fulfilled person I know, because I have faith and trust and love in The Lord God. Nothing is too hard for Him. Absolutely nothing.

My Prayer

> *God,*
>
> *Thank You for having solutions to problems I don't even know about yet. I'm just relieved that I don't have to be in charge of fixing everything that goes wrong in my life...especially the circumstances beyond my control (there are a lot of those).*
>
> *I lay every single fear, doubt, worry, and anxiousness at your feet. With my free will, I choose Your will above my own. Your ways are higher than my ways. Your love is greater than my love. Your solutions are better than my solutions.*

I'm very, very grateful that I have unshakable faith that You built inside me over a lifetime of showing me the way. Sorry I was a slow learner at times and stupidly stubborn more than I'd like to admit. I just think You're awesome and wonderful. I can never Thank You enough for being there for me every step of the way.

Amen.

Reliance

"Trust in The Lord with all your heart, and do not lean on your own understanding."
— Proverbs 3:5

"Trust in The Lord forever, for The Lord God is an everlasting rock."
— Isaiah 26:4

"Cast all your anxieties on him, because he cares for you."
— 1 Peter 5:7

The definition of reliance is the DEPENDENCE ON or TRUST in someone or something.

Do not think for one single second that God has abandoned you in the midst of your greatest suffering on this earth. You are serving a phenomenal purpose with your life. We get so focused on our earthly existence that we lose sight of our Everlasting Future.

We can't possibly undertake our biggest losses, tragedies, and seemingly hopeless situations on our own. Internally, in our hearts, we know that we must reach out in order to cope. The Lord God wants to be your rock.

I heard a story about a toddler that was blind, and he was laying down in his bed, literally face to face with his mother. He called out for his mother because he didn't see her. He thought he was alone, and he was afraid. His mother said, "I'm right here in front of you. I'm right here."

That is a perfect example of the closeness of God in our lives. We can't see Him but when we call His name, He is already with us.

"Call to me and I will answer you, and will tell you great and hidden things that you have not known."

— Jeremiah 33:3

From my own personal experience, I will tell you that when God speaks to your heart, you will be amazed and in awe of the things He wants to reveal to you. Let the word of God paint a picture in your mind of how your life will unfold. He doesn't break his promises. His word is truth. Seek Him, and you will find Him.

Reliance on Jesus will strengthen you during your biggest challenges. I learned that the more I completely surrendered, expressed my gratitude, and humbled myself before God, during my cancer pain and suffering, the more I felt God's presence in my life. His presence gives me the fortitude to walk in confidence… that yes… everything might not be ok right now, but relief and favor are coming…and they will come in abundance.

"But seek first the kingdom of God and his righteousness, and all these things will be added to you."

— Matthew 6:33

Empowerment

The hardest thing that I've had to let go of, in my life, is a sense of control. I say a sense of control versus actual control because we fool ourselves into thinking we have control over everything.

We 100% do not control things or people or circumstances. Need proof?..Natural disasters, death, disease, and free will.

I can't even eat breakfast or dinner or text or write these emails without being in pain. My right hand is swollen, numb, arthritic, and covered in nerve pain every morning and every night. I made God a promise that I intend to keep though. I will write about my life experience, tell the truth (even if it is embarrassing), and try to verbalize my spiritual growth.

I have no control over my sickness and its effects on my body. Yesterday, my face broke out with red pimples like bumps all over my cheeks and most of it disappeared overnight. My constant weight gain is discouraging.

I think I miss having energy the most. I have to remind myself that chemo kills my good cells too...not just the bad ones.

When all feels lost and I want to empower myself, I run to God. My latest new prayer is "Lord hear my heart." Sometimes, I'm too tired to pray, and I can't think clearly because my short-term memory is extremely bad.

When I can't find the words, I ask God to know my needs by examining my heart. I have no real control over my sickness... no control over my income...no control over the weather (rain is excruciating to my bone cancer), and no control over how other people treat me.

I run to God who has authority over everything. Even the stars and sun listen to Him. He is all powerful. When I need to feel empowered, I go to The Bible. God's word gives me strength.

When I pray, God's Mercy gives me Hope. When I obey, my commitment to God brings me joy, because I know it pleases Him.

I walk in gratitude, so I don't slip and fall into a valley of self pity.

I may not be in control, but I will forever love and be close to my Father, in Heaven, who has the power to make the impossible possible....Now that's empowerment!

I do not fight this cancer alone or helplessly.

"The Lord will fight for you, and you have only to be silent."

— Exodus 14:14

And What Does God Deserve?

It's all about *us* isn't it?

> *Our* comfort. *Our* good health. *Our* bigger, better stuff. *Our* damaged feelings and disappointments. *Our* success or failures. *Our* love lives. *Our* looks. *Our* youth. *Our* acceptance by everyone we come in contact with on this earth. What **we** want. When **we** want it. How much of it **we** deserve.

I deserve nothing more because I can't get a better gift than what I've already been given. Who else can promise me an ETERNITY of PEACE, BEAUTY, HAPPINESS, and LOVE? No one, but GOD.

Who else can grant you repetitive forgiveness when you really mess up? God's son, Jesus Christ, through His shed blood... for you... for all of us.

The better question to ask instead of "What do *we* deserve?" is "WHAT DOES GOD DESERVE?" What gift do we give Him in gratitude for what He has already given us? Loyalty? Obedience? Honor? Respect? Gratitude? Acknowledgement? Love?

I see it all the time; Tweaking behavior to please a person rather than the one that has your life in the palm of His hand. How often do we diminish our admiration for our Lord and Savior in front of others? Do we "dumb down" our Christianity at times according to our social situations to "fit in?" Are we silent when we should speak?

Do we change the music in our cars and homes according to who is coming over? Do we leave our Bibles out on the table for everyone to see, or do we put them away in a drawer? Do we at least try to save a soul we see in front of us that needs saving?

God doesn't reward our success; God rewards our effort. Deny Him now and prepare to be denied at your death. It's something to think about.

What does God deserve? We should be asking ourselves that question every single morning. Your answer could determine your eternal life. This earthly life is temporary. We are but skin and bones and tissue (and cancer) that wasn't meant to last forever.

Your own words and actions will be the ones that determine your future. Think about it. I'm not giving up my eternal life in paradise for anybody else's approval of me on this earth, period. Even with what I am enduring right now, I wouldn't trade places with anybody else's soul. I know where I'm headed.

"But whoever denies Me before men, I also will deny before my Father who is in Heaven."

— Matthew 10:33

Chapter 4

Be Still

Be Still and Know That I Am

"Be still, and know that I am God; I will be exalted among the nations, I will be exalted in the earth!"
— Psalm 26:10

Our lives are hectic these days. Whether it's work, children, social commitments, holidays, birthday celebrations, errands, yard work, housework or renovations, car issues, trips, paying a pile of bills, doctor appointments— it's a never ending to do list. I am the world's worst "list" person who tries to cram 100 things in every single day. Until this summer, I never just took a day off, and I mean an entire day off, from everything.

You don't realize how "connected" you are to the world until you totally disconnect from it. Electronically speaking — leaving your cell phone behind feels like handing your newborn baby to a stranger on the street. It's hard to do. Not checking emails is like being dropped via helicopter to a remote location with no vital supplies, "How will I survive?" Watching TV, reading the paper, or listening to the radio, surely there will be a natural disaster or some earth shattering celebrity break up, and I will be the last one to find out!

I'm surrounded (and suffocated) in my home by one project after another with no visible end in sight: ripping up the carpet, patching walls, painting, replacing fixtures and appliances, replacing floors and old furniture – you name it, and it needs an overhaul. I try to tackle it piece by piece because it has to get done, and I'm it in my household – no husband or boyfriend... just me.

None of the 100 "must get done" items bring me closer to God. The more I do, the more tired I become. Fatigue makes me numb. Work makes me numb. People pleasing activities make me numb. My spirit becomes dull.

God sits patiently on his throne looking upon me, and I finally hear his commanding voice through my dulled spirit,

"BE STILL and KNOW THAT I AM."

Who, me? The biggest wiggle worm on the planet? Be still?

The last time I didn't listen (I mean flat out ignored God), cancer forced me to lay in bed and be still. In pain is not the way to I want to experience stillness again... Sitting under a shady Palm Tree in the Bahamas watching the waves roll in completely by myself, now that is how I want to be still!

It's true you know – if you're still, I mean truly still, your mouth is still, your muscles are still, your whole body is still, and you disconnect yourself from all the ways of the world — you will actually be sitting right beside God.

You will know His presence in a powerful way. It's imperative to engage your spirit with STILLNESS sometimes. We are always talking, doing, and thinking. We hardly ever STOP completely. We view that as a waste of time. We want to be productive.

Yet, in our stillness, God can be heard more clearly, seen with more impact, and our spirit is no longer numb. Wouldn't that be our biggest accomplishment today and every day? To feel closer to God? To be awestruck by his creation? To happily just know that this is the day The Lord has made, rejoice and be glad in it?

When I'm on the beach, it never escapes me that I'm walking on the edge of a continent and looking out into an ocean that is vast beyond my comprehension.

Yes, read your Bible, devotionals, and go to church, but also walk outside and see what our mighty Father has CREATED. It's AMAZING!

I'm floored when I look around. You can see God EVERYWHERE if you will just sit still and expand your view. God is waiting for you to join Him. The laundry and dishes aren't going anywhere, and the world won't stop it's rotation if you take a day off to just be still.

My Prayer:

Father,

Thank You for creating so many things for me to enjoy. I would love to sit back, relax, and enjoy them with You. Sometimes, I forget to balance my life, and I get distracted. One day, I will have my entire life flash before my eyes. I want to remember my peaceful moments sitting in Your presence. I want to minimize my scurrying "worker ant" behavior, so I can grow closer to You. I realize when I put our relationship first, You will tie up all the other loose ends in my life. Your desire is to have all of my attention more than to see how productive I can be in a day. It is never a waste of time to be still. You amaze me every day and in every way.

Always, Your loving daughter

Amen.

I Sit in Awe

Sometimes we get so wrapped up in doing, that we forget to take a step back. We immerse ourselves in errands, work, family, projects, and just plain "busyness." I, myself, let my health swallow me from time to time, until I make an active decision to step back and reflect. During my quiet time this morning (always the best part of my day), I reflected on my accomplishments and what I've learned.

God's word is like a tidal wave for me. It has strength and power. It comes in like a lion at times, refusing to be ignored. I have to ride that tidal wave, submerging myself in its message. With anticipation, you are wondering, "What's that message?"

That's just it. In its entirety, it's hard to take it all in at the same time, but the entire Bible is that message; it is filled with promises, truths, love, healing, and answers to any problem you will ever face in this lifetime. I sit in awe of that concept, that truth. How great is that? God... the never ending provider of all things (just as He has promised in Numbers 23:19-20).

I am constantly being overtaken by amazement. God has changed people's hearts in my wake...people I couldn't conceive of ever changing. He spoke to my son when I thought my words were falling on deaf ears. He says no problem when I think there is no way. He has instantaneously provided solutions to big dilemmas and then said... "What's next?" He has plucked people out of my life who meant to do me harm. He has spoken to me...over and over again, through miracles and signs that I cannot ignore. He has taken my death certificate and ripped it up more than once. He has made me wise in ways I never thought possible...there's a peace that comes with seeing and knowing God. I wish for you to draw close to our Father so that you may know that peace (that surrounded me).

Put Him first.
The Kingdom of God awaits... paradise... home.
That's all I can say. Put Him first.

If you wrote a list of every single problem you have today and every situation that weighs heavily on your heart...look back at that list and ask yourself, "Which one of these is too big for my God to handle?" You already know the answer.

Step back from your busyness of doing, worrying, and dreading. Sit in awe at the foot of your Father and just thank Jesus for rescuing you from this weary world. His blood is on your doorstep...you are saved! Walk through this Sunday as if it were your last day on earth. Let go of pettiness, for God needs your whole heart and soul... not distracted, shattered pieces of it.

My Prayer

> *Lord, I pray that You hug these people today for me. Smile down on them. Remind us that we are Yours, and may we, with our whole hearts and our free will, choose You for eternity.*

Amen.

> *"So ever since we first heard about you we have kept on praying and asking God to help you understand what he wants you to do; asking him to make you wise about spiritual things; and asking that the way you live will always please The Lord and honor Him, so that you will always be doing good, kind things for others, while all the time you are learning to know God better and better. We are praying, too, that you will be filled with his mighty, glorious strength so that you can keep going no matter what happens -always full of the joy of The Lord, and always thankful to the Father who has made us fit to share all the wonderful things that belong to those who live in the kingdom of light. For he has rescued us out of the darkness and gloom of Satan's kingdom and brought us into the kingdom of His dear Son, who bought our freedom with his blood and forgave us all our sins."*
> — Colossians 1:9-14

Chapter 5

Father's Love

He Loves You

"...He [Jesus] who came down from heaven...even so must the Son of Man be lifted up, that whoever believes in Him should not perish but have eternal life. For God so loved the world that He gave His only begotten Son, that whoever believes in Him should not perish but have everlasting life. For God did not send His Son into the world to condemn the world, but that the world through Him might be saved."

— John 3:13-17

When we love people, we are accepting all the parts of that other person...good and bad.

The only problem with people loving us is, we never show them every part of us. It would be impossible really...to share every thought, every fear, every experience you've ever had over a lifetime. Only God sees you in your entirety. He sees your dreams, your hopes, your fears, and anxieties. He sees the ugly parts of you that would embarrass you...the parts of hatred, doubt, anger, and resentment. I always say that God knows who we are in the dark. We show the world the parts we want them to see. God sees the raw and exposed us from every angle...our inside hidden parts.

The Good News: HE LOVES YOU!!! He sees ALL of you and He loves you unconditionally. Who else but God accepts you just the way you are? I've often wondered why people can't or won't accept that love from Him. I'm guessing they think it's "too good to be true" or that they are "undeserving." It makes me sad when people deny themselves God's unconditional love. The best decision of my entire life has been to let God love me...To let Him in my heart...To receive not what I deserve, but what God freely gives...HIS LOVE.

May you all be willing to let Him love you today. He seeks a relationship with you. He has unending love to give you that never fails, never runs out, and nothing can ever separate you from it.

> *"And I am convinced that nothing can ever separate us from God's love. Neither death nor life, neither angels nor demons, neither our fears for today nor our worries about tomorrow — not even the powers of hell can separate us from God's Love."*
>
> — Romans 8:38

> *"But because of His great love for us, God, who is rich in mercy, made us alive with Christ even when we were dead in transgressions - it is by grace you have been saved."*
>
> — Ephesians 2:4-5

> *"For God so loved the world that He gave His one and only Son, that whoever believes in Him shall not perish but have eternal life."*
>
> — John 3:16

God Is Merciful

God grants us mercy and a fresh start every single day of our lives. He doesn't expect payment for that mercy because the price has already been paid. I don't know about you, but I really need that mercy, on an ongoing basis. God, cover me in that mercy!!!!

We have the choice of being merciful to others or making them pay a price to receive our mercy. Hmmmmm....what do we do with that? Do we want others to suffer, because they made us suffer? They were bad to us, so we need to get angry, talk about them, get even, and retaliate. That doesn't sound very Christian does it? What if God treated us the way we treat others?

When someone hurts us, we should actually talk GENUINE kindness to them (their own guilt will eventually overtake them). We should flat out do nice things for others (especially when it's inconvenient or difficult for us, because that shows God our true motives and that we didn't take the easy road).

Forgiveness is mercy. Doing for others and giving to others is mercy. Being the first to reach out is extending mercy.

Mercy on our part makes us more Christlike (and that grants us the favor of others and God).

"Try to show as much compassion as your Father does. Never criticize or condemn-or it will all come back on you. Go easy on others; then they will do the same for you. For if you give, you will get! Your gift will return to you in full and overflowing measure, pressed down, shaken together to make room for more, and running over. Whatever measure you use to give— large or small — will be used to measure what is given back to you."
                                                              — Luke 6:36-38

I wrote this today because I'm grateful for God's mercy in my life. I also wrote this because I've had others hurt me in very big ways. I'm astounded at how mean they have been to me. It is because of the Holy Spirit that I can see my own shortcomings and convict myself to be a better Christian....to not be like them and to not let their words or actions poison my soul.

I'm guilty of partial forgiveness and mercy. It is only through the grace of God that I am compelled to continue to strive to go beyond the minimum and show forgiveness and mercy to others.

I'm not perfect, but I'm striving to do better every day. In all honesty, I have a ways to go, but I'm working on it.

My Prayer

> *God,*
>
> *Thank You for granting me mercy. Thank You that even when I slip one day, You allow me to start fresh the next. Your forgiveness cleans my soul.*
>
> *I truly want to extend mercy to others because it grows my spirit in wonderful ways. I need Your help to do that. I want people to be able to see YOUR loving heart through MY actions. Help me rise above my usual tendencies or bad habits through the example set by Your son, Jesus. I want to do better. When others speak of me, I want them to be able to use the word merciful in their description of me.*
>
> *I can't change my past but I can shape my future through You and by You!*
>
> *Your Growing Child,*
>
> *Amen.*

Incomprehensible Love

During times of great suffering and loss, this message may seem hard to believe, so it's important to plant it in your souls before you are tempted to question the Wondrous plan of your creator. In sickness and in health...in death and in birth...you are LOVED. Every day, keep it on your lips and hold it in your heart.

> *"We are so preciously loved by God that we cannot even comprehend it. No created being can ever know how much and how sweetly and tenderly God loves them."*
>
> — Julian of Norwich

My Prayer

Pour out Your love upon me today, God, for I am struggling just to survive. I am without sleep and weak from my long term suffering. I look to You for rescue and blessing. I trust You with all my heart to make what seems like a hopeless situation turn into something amazing. I have not and will not give up because I know....not only Your power, but Your unlimited love for me.

I close my eyes and remember days that I used to run and feel the sun on my face and fresh air in my lungs. I miss those days a lot as I look at the world through my bedroom window. It would be easy for me to think You have forgotten me sometimes.

I know You chose me specifically to help other strugglers remember that a God who created us would never seek to destroy His own creation.

I promise to look at what's right in my life instead of what's wrong. When I fall off the path meant for me, all I ask is that You pick me back up and carry me the rest of the way. I love You. Thank You for loving me more than I can even understand.

Amen.

Chapter 6

God's Delays Are Not His Denials

Expections and God's Timetable

> *"The hard prayer is simply this: God may YOUR WILL be done. The reason that prayer is hard is because, somewhere in our head, we fear His will might not line up with our wishes. His will might not be the quick easy road we were hoping for. What if His will tests us in ways we don't want to be tested?"*
>
> — Teresa Koska

I've often told my son that God is not a magic genie. You don't rub the lamp and ask for three wishes when you pray, then expect God to meet your demands immediately. God wasn't ushered into existence for us. At one time or another, we are all guilty of expecting things to revolve around our time table.

If I'm really being honest, I fully expected God to swoop in at any time and take away my cancer in the middle of it so the doctors would be dumbfounded by the miracle. I went to bed every night praying that prayer, and I would truthfully expect the next appointment at Duke to be my miracle appointment.

That was MY EXPECTATION but not God's answer – HIS WAY. HIS TIME. HIS PLAN. HIS MIRACLE. You see, God created us, therefore, God gets to decide.

Last night, I won the top division volleyball tournament in doubles with my co-ed partner. We were not playing very well in the first round and barely squeaked by in the second. My partner could not get a serve in to save his life, and he was setting me all over the place. My shoulder and knee were bothering me, so I wasn't hitting or moving on the court very fast. Then, in the finals, we brought the thunder! We revised our strategy, both scoring several points off ace serves and had some fantastic defense as we really listened to each other's calls to get the points off hits. We were a team in every sense of the word. We said, no matter what happens, we are going to encourage each other, and if we make a mistake, we will focus on the next point even harder to make up for it. Did I mention we played the team that had beaten us several times during the regular season? We won when it counted!

God steps into your life when it is the Perfect Time to do so. When He does, it is powerful, you can literally feel a huge shift. Last night, it wasn't just me and my partner playing in the finals, we had God with us. It is incredible to experience a breath from God. You have this inner confidence that no one else can dampen.

Our expectation should not be that our desires are met, but that God will provide for us what we need, when we need it, and on His terms.

Even if we lost last night or cancer took me home, it would still be the right thing at the right time because my Father knows what is best. I don't want you to give up on whatever struggle you are going through because your answer isn't coming fast enough from God. He will come through in a very powerful way when the time is right. Your miracle is coming – your hard earned victory is right around the corner!

God Never Sleeps

"The Lord is watching everywhere and keeps his eye on both the evil and the good."

— Proverbs 15:13

It's amazing when you think about it. Every time we go to sleep, God stays awake and is watching over every single one of us all over the world. Every single second of every single day, He is awake watching, answering our prayers, protecting us, and teaching us. It never stops, ever. It comforts me to know that.

Sometimes, God gets blamed for letting evil exist or not stopping it before it happens. We live in a broken world that generations helped create. God did create a perfect world free from evil – it's called Heaven. He has given all of us an open invitation to live there with him one day. We just need to RSVP.

I'm a firm believer that everything happens for a reason. Good and Bad. Know this, if it is good, it is from God. If it is bad (evil), God can and will turn it around for the greater good.

I know what you are thinking, "What about all the awful things that have happened to me, those I love, and things reported on the news?" The evil one exists in this world; it is his playground so to speak, so he won't be satisfied until he destroys everything. God has a different plan altogether. He wants to love you beyond measure. Make sure you invest your time with the One who created you, not the one who will do anything to destroy your happiness and health.

Our watchful Father is awake; He's listening 24 hours a day. Talk to Him as often as you can, and tell Him everything on your mind and things that weigh heavy on your heart. RSVP right now.

Even if you have accepted Jesus as your Lord and Savior in the past, tell God again that you choose His ways daily and want His guidance while you are living in this temporary place. Ask for His protection from evil. Thank Him for keeping a watchful eye over you.

Nothing can ever separate you from God's love...that is HIS promise.

My Prayer

Thank You, God, for never saying, "Whoops," or "I didn't see that coming." You see all and know all. I am grateful that You never sleep. I am grateful that You never leave me to fend for myself on this earth without You. I am grateful that You created an eternal resting place where evil cannot exist. Wrap me in bubble wrap until I can get there! I want to RSVP.

I accept Your son Jesus Christ as my Lord and Savior. Forgive my sins Father. I choose You every day in every way. I want to live with You for eternity.

Amen.

"No" Means "No"

NO! How many times have you heard that word come out of your own mouth? My son tries to bargain and argue with me after I tell him no.

"Just 15 more minutes mom. Can I play a computer game, if I do chores? All the other kids in my class have one. Why not?"

I would love to hear him enthusiastically say, "Yes ma'am, you know what's best for me." Ha ha ha ha ha! I could barely even write that because on what planet would that ever happen? Let's be real.

I'm God's child and sometimes, He tells me no. I'm the kid that asks for the same thing over and over and over again hoping for a different response.

"But God, I don't want to be alone. Why can't I have my soulmate? How about this week? Is it time yet? I'm lonely. I'm tired of being held prisoner to sickness. I'm ready to be done right now. I don't want to suffer anymore. Can today be my last sick day? I'm ready for the next chapter in my life. Can I start today?"

No?

"Buuuuuuuuttttttt Godddddd, all your other children have that. Why not me?"

"Because I SAID NO... and no, means no."

I should be saying, "Yes sir, You know what's best for me."

So, here I am pouting... the answer is no. It's hard to accept because I want something else (just like a spoiled child). I have to resist the urge to bargain, argue, and question (Not like any of that would work with God anyway). As a matter of fact, I'm sure He finds that quite irritating.

I guess, the cat's out of the bag, I am quite stubborn. What can I say? The heart wants what the heart wants. Sometimes, we have to accept that God tells us no. We don't always get what we want when we want it. Just know that when God tells us "No," it always comes from a caring place of protection.

A work in progress... trying desperately not to be spoiled...

P.S. Eventually, the answer is YES, but in His good and perfect timing.

God's Perfect Timing

Let me start this by saying, I just may be one of the most impatient people on the planet!

I look at microwaves and say, "Really!? You can't go any faster? I have things to do!" I get irritated when people unwrap presents super slowly because they want to save the paper; inside my head I'm thinking, "I will just buy you a roll of the wrapping paper if you like it that much" (and keep in mind that I recycle everything, but it still irritates me).

Disclaimer: Sorry all you unwrapping slowpokes out there, cancer only made my impatience grow stronger because time is so valuable to me now.

Now here's the part where I tell you a few years ago that God stepped in my life and showed me in an unquestionable way just how perfect His timing is.

I spilled coffee on my clothes (bummer, I know) forcing me to have to change. Afterwards, when I was finally in the car ready to go, I noticed that I forgot to grab my bag. Then, I was distracted while driving, and I missed an important turn. This put me back five minutes which was only made worse as I hit every single red light in town. Is that even possible? Well, I certainly found out that it was. Then, I couldn't find a parking space at my friend's place.

All of those things...right down to the very last second were extremely important.

Why? Because it put me at the scene of a hit and run accident at the very moment I needed to be there. She was literally still rolling on the pavement after being hit.

To make a long story short, all those irritating things that tried my patience and made me "late" actually made me right on time for something more important.

I carry that with me every day. All the things that may seem unimportant in your day, right down to every single little nuisance, are not as they appear. God is lining things up towards a goal that you can't see. Don't question them. Just accept that everything really does happen for a reason, and if God has His Hand in it, it's a very good reason.

His timing is perfect, right down to the exact second!

I know sometimes we get tired of waiting for things to happen.... believe me...I know. I know that if we are being honest with ourselves, we get irritated that things aren't happening on our time table.

> *How long do we have to wait? When will that right man come into my life? When will my financial difficulties be over? When will I stop being sad over losing that person or animal in my life? When will my body recover from my injury or sickness? When will I be caught up? When will I stop worrying about my child? When will that mean person get it and start being friendly? When will my ship come in so to speak?*

I have your answer to every single one of those questions!

The answer is when God deems it the PERFECT time. He doesn't just pacify us like spoiled children because we want things (no matter how badly we want them). The final outcome in all our situations is in His Hands. Forcing a microwave to work faster isn't going to happen, no matter how much I tap my foot waiting impatiently.

> *"We can make our plans, but the final outcome is in God's hands."*
> — Proverbs 16:1

66

Peace of spirit and mind come from letting those words sink in. If you struggle, it's because you are fighting against that knowledge.

"Let go and let God" is a catchy phrase, but essentially in basic terms, God can and will "handle it."

I have to pray for patience; it does not come naturally to me at all! I also have to be reminded of God's perfect timing, so every once in a while He will jerk a knot in me to open my eyes. I have learned that the more I give up to Him, the more my life blooms in miraculous ways.

May His ways and His timing chase you down today so your life can bloom too.

Perfect Timing

Timing is everything isn't it?

I have spent the last three days at home with a sick child. He is on his second round of antibiotics and hopefully will return to school tomorrow. He actually apologized to me for being sick, and I told him everything happens for a reason.

Maybe God wants to protect us from a car wreck or a gas leak that's on the way to school. Maybe God specifically needs me to stay home because there's something far more important to learn here than out in the world.

Maybe my son needed to realize he has a parent he can depend on, as I will drop everything (whenever and wherever) and cancel every appointment to tend to him. As a mother, that is my job. Lots of moms out there get that! It helps me appreciate my mom for taking care of me when I was sick, that's for sure!

Maybe it's to teach my son a work ethic that he can only get from having to make up all that school work.

Maybe it was to rekindle a relationship with a caring next door neighbor who brought food over.

I could literally come up with a hundred reasons why being sick is a good thing. God's healing hands will reach down and heal when the time is right.

His perfect plan will unfold sometimes right before our very eyes with obvious understanding. Other times, His plan will unfold while we are sleeping and behind someone else's closed door (in the life of someone that we've never even met who was impacted by something we said or did). You see, God can take your leftovers, using a little of this and a little of that, to make a beautiful tinfoil swan (trying to make a visual connection for you). In other words, what we see as something that is a "WHY ME?" moment or a "WHAT AM I SUPPOSED TO DO WITH THIS?" moment in our lives, God would say, "Hold on, I'm not done yet."

My advice for the day (from a girl who has been there and has season tickets), quit looking at your watch expecting God to make sense of your situation in the now, on your timing. Your time would be better spent growing, maturing, and evolving in the middle of what you're experiencing; it's the only way to move forward more quickly. Look for the good in the bad; it makes the bad not just bearable but intentional on a positive level. The key is to remember that everything God has planned for you is for your greater good - That bears repeating:

EVERYTHING God has PLANNED for YOU is for YOUR GREATER GOOD. The minute you stop resisting and fighting Him on every turn is the minute the process moves at a quicker pace: let God have at it! If you need examples of His PERFECT PLAN and PERFECT TIMING, just think of the story of how we met. Remember that day? That time in your life? We were introduced at the exact right time. The Bible is crammed full of perfect timing examples.

Everything happens for a reason and at the exact time it should. Nothing is a surprise to God. He is literally waiting for you to come to Him, and He has a solution to every single problem you will ever face. Day and Night, without rest, God continually plans for your greater good. Trust in that.

Just remember, when you get frustrated, don't understand, and feel like nothing is changing in the direction you want to go in, picture God speaking directly to you saying, "Hold on, I'm not done yet. The timing has to be perfect. You've been waiting for hours, days, weeks, months, years, and I have been working on your purpose and plan much longer than that— before you even came into existence."

In Due Time

"Humble yourselves, therefore, under God's mighty hand, that He may lift you up in due time."

— 1 Peter 5:6

This is going to be one of those emails where I'm going to be really blunt. People can be thoughtless, selfish, hurtful, and just plain mean and cruel. It's bad when you don't know them... Worse when it's a friend... Bottom line is they can cut you to the quick with their actions and make you cry your heart out with their vicious words.

What does God say about this unwanted situation when you are in the thick of it? In due time, He will be your justice. I would love to tell you that it will happen in your lifetime and you can relish the fact that they are "getting what they deserve" for hurting you. That's not the way of God.

Humble means to have or show a modest or low estimate of ONE'S OWN IMPORTANCE. Hmmmm. I guess to translate I would say: get over yourself. Submit to God's will. Let him handle them as He sees fit. When the time is right, you will have your day in the sun. To wish them the same suffering they inflicted on you, is not the way a child of God should behave.

Are they right to hurt you? Nope.
Do you wish they would change their ways? Yep.
Is it unfair? At this moment, it definitely is.
Will they pay for their behavior? In Due Time.

I wouldn't trade places with a single cold hearted hater if you paid me a million bucks. My eternal salvation is worth more than that! I've read about the wrath of God. I will do whatever it takes to get off His naughty list. That's not where you want to be.

70

You want to be the one getting lifted up by God's hand...not getting demolished under it. Pity those who hurt you. Pray even for God to grant them mercy, as odd as that may sound, for that is the same mercy that you will want for yourself one day when it is your turn to sit in the seat of judgment.

P.S. I am truly sorry for a single moment that anyone dimmed the light of your spirit. You don't deserve that. No one does. In due time, your light will never grow dim.

There Is Nothing Wrong
With the Word, "No"

For the longest time I was the "Yes Girl." I wanted to make everybody happy. Making everybody else happy came at a very high personal cost. For me, it was my health, social life, family, and quiet time with God took a hit.

I can't go back and recover all the time I lost on pleasing people who now wouldn't even cross the street to bring me a cup of soup. That's truly even beside the point. The biggest problem with saying, "Yes" to everyone, is the amount of time and energy you spend away from God.

What about God? He deserves to be first! Think about this. "No" may sting for a little while when you say it to someone, but your TRUE FRIENDS and LOVING FAMILY MEMBERS want what's best for you and not their own selfish needs.

I had to tell one of my friends that a long time ago. It's ok to tell me no. I won't leave you or get mad at you. I won't love you any less. Sometimes, you just can't do it. I would rather somebody tell me, "No," and tell God, "Yes." Instead of taking the time for me... take the time for Him. It's time to get your priorities straight.

Every time you say yes...what are you investing your time in? What will it cost you? Is it really something you want to do, or do you just feel guilty and obligated? How far out have you obligated yourself to the point of dread? It's a horrible feeling to look at your calendar and realize you said, "Yes" to too many things and you would much rather be nourishing your mind, body, and spirit with that time.

God did not intend us to make decisions that are based on fear or guilt. He intended us to make decisions based on love.

Love for Him. Love for ourselves. Love for others. Question your motives before saying, "Yes."

If you worry about the aftermath of saying, "No," let God fight your battles!!! It is never a bad decision to spend your time with God. When you put Him in first place in your life, everything else will fall into place the way that it should.

It took me a long time to wake up to this realization. It's a much BETTER LIFE. I pray you all will practice saying "NO" to the distractions of the world and "YES" to more time building a relationship with God.

Chapter 7

Christ Before Us

Walking Before Us

"What then shall we say to these things? If God is for us, who can be against us?"
— Romans 8:31

I find myself, once again, in bed recovering from my latest Chemo round, three stomach injections for my bone marrow, and 42 clinical trial drug pills. My skin breaks out in hot red splotches, especially on my face. I'm already losing feeling in my hands and feet again. My vision is becoming temporarily blurry. Every bone in my body hurts from the inside out. I'm really really tired, and I know the flu-like symptoms will start tonight. My taste buds are going numb, and food has begun to lose its flavor. My jaw hurts, and I'm hoping the mouth sores can skip me this round. I had almost forgotten how bad this feels..... almost.

As I'm laying in bed, I'm thinking of all the prayers I've said about this cancer. So many prayers. I get to the point that I don't know what's left to be said. I know God already knows how I feel and my heart's desire to stay on this earth. I know He knows that I have a son and friends and family that I don't want to leave behind. I know He knows I'm tired of suffering.

Then it dawned on me, God isn't waiting for my prayer. He has already prepared everything for my future. He walked ahead of me long before I even knew I had cancer. Nothing is a surprise to Him. It's ok not to have the right words when I talk to Him. I just need to grasp the concept that He's in control, and I need to let my confidence grow when I remember that.

My Prayer

God,

In the beginning, You created all things. You have been present since the dawn of time, and with You, there is no end. You are all-knowing. You are everywhere at once...including ahead of where I'm at in my life right now. You not only walk with me, You walk before me. Thank You for making all the preparations.

Thank You for knowing what I think and understanding how I feel yesterday, today, and all the tomorrows that I haven't even begun to think about yet. I know You love me. I know You want the best for me.

As I rest and heal and cry and pray, I want You to know I'm still confident in your plan for my life. Wherever I am, as long as I'm with You, I know it's going to be better than ok. It's going to be just perfect because You are perfect.

Blessed be Your wonderful name,

Amen.

What's Jesus up to Today?

If I called and asked you, "What are you up to today?" I'm pretty sure you would run down a "to-do list." Maybe you have gifts to buy, meals to cook, dropping something off, picking things up, cleaning your house, or maybe you have a meeting with someone. I'm sure it's a busy, busy day.

Imagine for a second if you gave Jesus a call and said, "Hey Jesus, what are You up to today?" Can you even imagine His response???

In the Bible it says this:

"For Christ did not enter a sanctuary made with human hands that was only a copy of the true one; he entered heaven itself, now to appear for us in God's presence."

— Hebrews 9:4

"Who then will condemn us? No one- for Christ Jesus died for us and was raised to life for us, and he is sitting in the place of honor at God's right hand, pleading for us."

— Romans 8:34

It bears repeating...FOR US.

Jesus is in Heaven right now pleading with God on OUR behalf. Pleading is a strong word.

As we go about our daily routines (most likely saying or doing a few things that would not please God), Jesus is beside our Father asking Him to give us another chance.

"Give them more time Father. Forgive them Father. Help them Father. She needs your intervention today. He needs your protection. Your children need healing. They need your mercy, your grace, your favor. Please forgive them. I paid

their price of salvation."

Can you imagine? We are loved continually.

We often think of Christ's birth (that time of year and all). We often think of His death (I still can't see a reenactment without crying). We think of His teachings recorded in the Bible (which I'm still learning from every day). But, how often do you think about what He is doing today, right this minute? How does it feel to have the best advocate you could possibly have in heaven? Daily, He is at God's right hand in heaven having conversations with God about us!

Here are the implications of that:

1. You are important to Jesus.

2. You are on His mind today.

3. You are forgiven by Jesus' sacrifice and His request to His Father when you ask for forgiveness.

4. You are LOVED by Jesus.

Somehow, a little itty-bitty thank you and back at ya' from us seems woefully inadequate. I sincerely believe the reason God hasn't demolished the earth completely to start over yet is because Jesus has begged Him to give us more time— more time so more souls would know and love God.

After all, Jesus was brought into this world to save it! Knowing all of that kind of makes my to-do list a little different on a daily basis. Now, I seek first the kingdom of God and trust Him with the rest of it. He's given us another day. So, what will you do with yours?

If you could call Jesus on the phone right now and speak with Him... what would you say? You can call Him right now and talk with Him...that's what prayer is. What's even cooler is HE ALWAYS ANSWERS your call...it never goes to voicemail! Don't have time for a phone call? Want to send him a text? That's ok too. Prayers don't have to be 15 minute conversations, short is ok too. He just wants you to stay in touch!

Nothing Goes Unnoticed

I want you to know that God sees everything.

You may feel neglected sometimes when you give your all and no one seems to acknowledge your hard work or sacrifice. You may be doing everything in your power to uphold the right principles even when you end up getting the short end of the stick in return. You may feel that your road has been extremely hard and life's not been very fair to you. People use you. People lie to your face. People let you down and stab you in the back even though you've only shown them kindness.

God is watching. He sees. Nothing goes unnoticed. He feels your injustice. He feels your frustration. He knows your anger, disappointment, and sadness.

Know that we serve a God of justice. He hasn't forgotten you. Those that mean you harm cannot escape His watchful eye. They can't hide in the dark. God lights up the dark. God sees behind closed doors. God sees every private thought. God sees every heart with clarity and whether they are motivated by good or evil. He sees. He knows. He acts. Make no mistake. He WILL act, but in His perfect timing.

As you walk through this day, know with certainty that God is ever watchful of every aspect of your life and every single person that you come in contact with. Nothing you do or say or think goes unnoticed by Him. The same goes for your enemies. That should be reassuring to you. He's got your back.

God Is Detail Oriented

Have you ever paused to think about how many details surround you?

I love every single shade of blue and green (I call them ocean colors). Pinecones are very interesting when you consider the layers of overlapping points almost like a flower. The weather outside is measured in degrees and is different everywhere you go..there is no uniformity. Brrrr...in Alaska. Whew....in the Bahamas. Every gorgeous flower smells vastly different. My favorite scents come from gardenias, peonies, hyacinth, and freesia. I love how some things shine and sparkle...like candlelight, mercury glass, and diamonds. In an orchestra, each instrument is interesting on its own and magnificent when joined together. I'm constantly amazed that music can still be arranged in new ways.

My point is...God didn't just churn out all the things we enjoy without great attention to detail. He thought about shapes, colors, sounds, textures, smells, and He even thought about how things evolve. We don't come into this world full grown. We have individual brains with different capacities for learning and growing. There is no denying that God is detail oriented.

When you came into this world, God spent a great deal of time on you: What family you would belong to. Your face. Your smile. Food preferences and all your likes and dislikes. Your heart. Who you would meet over a lifetime. Your talents. Your hurdles. Your triumphs. Your future plans. Your enormous purpose.

YOU ARE SPECIAL. VERY SPECIAL. Undeniably, the world needs your presence. Knowing the amount of thought that was put into making you should not only build your confidence, but elevate your sense of being loved. You are loved by your maker unconditionally.

YOU ARE LOVED FOREVER AND BEYOND MEASURE.

Think about what makes you different from those around you. Those differences are the tools/gifts that God gave you specifically to serve your life's purpose. Embrace your differences. They are the details that God knew long ago that would make you stand out and be heard. My stage four cancer did not come as a surprise to God. It's not a small detail in my life story...it's a huge one.

I have every confidence that God has prepared every detail of my beginning, my middle, and my end. Thank you God for not overlooking me or any other sufferer. I will not let this sickness be in vain. Thank you for showing me the deepest gratitude I've ever known for the good things in my life.

I hope and pray none of you sweep your difficulties under the rug to "move on." Look closer at the details in your circumstances that are meant to help you grow spiritually and influence others in positive ways. The real tragedy in life is when we view our life through our own eyes, instead of God's eyes and His intention for our temporary life on earth.

"What shall we say about such wonderful things as these? If God is for us, who could ever be against us? Since he did not spare even his own Son but gave him up for us all, won't he also give us everything else? Who dares accuse us whom God has chosen for his own? No one - for God himself has given us right standing with himself. Who then will condemn us? No one - for Christ Jesus died for us and was raised to life for us, and he is sitting in the place of honor at God's right hand pleading for us." Can anything ever separate us from Christ's love? Does it mean He no longer loves us if we have trouble or calamity, or are persecuted, or hungry, or destitute, or in danger, or threatened with death? As the scriptures say, "For your sake we are killed every day; we are being slaughtered like sheep. No, despite all these things overwhelming victory is ours through Christ, who loved us. And I am convinced that nothing can ever separate us from God's love. Neither

death nor life, neither angels nor demons, neither our fears
for today nor our worries about tomorrow – not even the
powers of hell can separate us from God's love. No power in
the sky above or in the earth below – indeed, nothing in all
creation will ever be able to separate us from the love of God
that is revealed in Christ Jesus our Lord."

— Romans 8:31-39

Wowsa!

Impressive! There are no accidents or coincidences, only details leading us in the right direction to know and experience deep LOVE.

Do not be afraid of your problems. Keep your thoughts aligned with your purpose, and God will rescue you. My trust keeps growing in the midst and depth of my own personal death sentence. I know the truth and the truth is good. With the attention to detail and care that God has given to everything He has ever made…I stand tall knowing how carefully He has planned the outcome of my life (Your life too!).

How Christ's Power Is Made Perfect

I have made it through a full boxing match. I surpassed ten rounds (of treatment and chemo). Every time I got knocked down hard, I got back up and faced cancer. POW...in the head. BAM...in the chest. BLINDSIDED...in the spine. UGH... right in the stomach. I've had headaches, blurry vision, pain, and nausea. I got back up. I got back up, faced my opponent with trembling legs, and stood my ground. I didn't win, but I lasted. As a matter of fact, I wanted to stop getting up the last few rounds and surrender. I'm tired and weaker than I've ever been. I've said the begging prayers. I've said the pleading prayers.

"God, I'm too weak. If You want me to live, You will have to step in and take over. I have been broken down to nothing. I have nothing left....my strength is all gone. All the poison in my body has robbed me of my vitality. Help me. I need You. I can't do this by myself."

This, of course, becomes my "turn the corner prayer." Why? Because God gives His perfect grace, power, and love to those who are weak. He shines and does His best work when we are TOTALLY DEPENDENT on Him. After praying that prayer, I was literally covered in love the following day. Everyone reached out to me wanting to make my life better...easier. People called, texted, and I was sent cards with encouraging words. That is no coincidence. That is God answering me.

> *"But he said to me, "My grace is sufficient for you, for MY POWER IS MADE PERFECT IN WEAKNESS." Therefore I will boast all the more gladly of my weaknesses, so that the Power of Christ may rest upon me."*
>
> — 2 Corinthians 12:9

I get this now. I really didn't get it before. I was too independent and self-sufficient to need Christ 100%. I bet, if you are being honest with yourself, you would have to admit that you have rarely come before God in complete weakness, so that His power is made perfect in your life. I would need Christ, when I couldn't do or have or achieve something occasionally. I needed Him, when I felt something was beyond my reach, but not HIS reach. I needed Him when I decided it was time to pray or turn my attention to Him to fix a problem. I have loved Him faithfully, without question, but I have never given Him everything. I have never been this weak before. I had to TOTALLY surrender everything to Him. I was so weak, I couldn't get back up. Now I can boldly say...I'm not so tough. I'm not so brave. I'm easily injured and my feelings are easily hurt. I am weak beyond description. And yet.... I'm complete in my fulfillment because Christ has rested His Power upon me yet again.

When I boast.... I boast in The Lord. I'm still here and still fighting because of His Grace... Because of His Favor... Because of His Power. In my weakness, His Power is made PERFECT. It's true when they say that we are our own worst enemy. Do not deny yourself The Power of God in your life because you think you are strong enough to go forward alone in any endeavor. The weaker you are, the stronger you can be. Through hardships, trials, and adversities, our faith and total reliance on God can make us stronger beyond anything we ever dreamed possible. I look back on my year of cancer so far and know I didn't get back up on my own. Christ picked me up and nurtured my body and spirit to the point that I had more than enough, every single round, to make it through. He took my hopelessness and discouragement and transformed them into strength.

I pray you will let Christ transform you in all your weaknesses. Let Him take the reins 100%. You are missing out when you live your life based upon what you can do and provide for yourself. You will never feel more loved than when you let Christ Himself love you perfectly.

He Is Here For You

I Gave You...

> "Therefore do not worry, saying, 'What shall we eat?' or 'What shall we drink?' or 'What shall we wear?' For after all these things the Gentiles seek. For your heavenly Father knows that you need all these things. But seek first the kingdom of God and His righteousness, and all these things shall be added to you."
>
> — Matthew 6:31-33

When I try to think of things from God's perspective, it's hard not to be grateful. If I sat and had a conversation with Him, I picture it going something like this...

God:

"I gave you sunrises and sunsets. You took in a few, but you didn't make a point of seeing more. I painted new ones for you every day."

"I gave you a perfectly functioning body, and for the longest time you only used just a portion of its strength."

"I gave you friends, and you put busy work before spending time with them even though I told you that I would supply your needs."

"I gave you answers, and you continue to ask me questions like you haven't understood My Word."

"I gave you miracles, and yet sometimes you still doubt how far my power reaches and what I'm capable of."

"I gave you a guardian angel to protect you. This angel is with you 24 hours a day from the time you are born until the day you come home to live with me. Yet sometimes, you fear what the future brings."

"I gave you free will, and you act like you have no choices to determine your own happiness."

"I gave you a beautiful soul, a bit of light from my own soul, and yet, you worry about what others think of your hair and face and body. You are beautiful just the way you are."

"I gave you my only Son, and some days you are sad and don't feel loved. How could I possibly love you more?"

"I gave you everything good you have ever enjoyed. Every smile, every laugh, every expression of love and forgiveness. Those things came from me."

"I gave you presents that you didn't even open because you were too self absorbed to find them."

"I gave you life on earth and an eternal life that is yours to claim."

"Don't overlook my goodness. Don't wish or long for things you think you are missing out on. Don't believe the lies that Satan tempts you with. I gave you everything to enrich your life and soul. Occasionally, I allowed things to be removed from your life, so you would learn about appreciation and how earthly things are temporary. I gave you my never ending compassion, mercy and unfailing grace during

those moments of loss. I gave you Hope that can only come from me. I gave you Healing that can only come from me. I gave you Comfort and Peace that can only come from me."

"When you prayed to Me, I listened to every precious word. When you praised me, I smiled. When you depended on me, I set a plan in motion for good things to come. When you said you wanted a relationship with me, I embraced your choice by preparing a place for you in my kingdom. When you shared my goodness, I heard music from your heart. I gave you my blessings because you are my child, and I delight in being your Father."

<u>Me</u>:

"I just love You beyond words. I want to be with You always. Thank You for Your gifts to me."

Provision and Protection

"For your ways are in full view of The Lord, and He examines all your paths."

— Proverbs 5:21

God sees, hears, and knows everything about us...every detail of every day. Nothing is a surprise to Him. The reason He can meet all of our needs is because of that personal knowledge of our daily lives (past, present, and future). It should comfort you to know that He uses that knowledge to meet our needs: provision and protection. Even with our free will, He sees the paths we choose and all of the pitfalls that lie ahead.

Who better to protect us?

Who better to provide what we will need for our journey?

My Prayer

Thank You, Father, that nothing is beyond Your reach. Thank You for caring about each one of us so intimately. Thank You for being our armor and protection against everything meant to do us harm. Thank You that we don't have to worry about our basic needs, because You have us covered. Thank You for seeing further ahead than we are able to.

Your ways are always the best ways. Lead us down the safest paths and bless us with knowing Your will for our lives.

Amen.

You Are Not Inconveniencing God

I am guilty of praying on a necessary basis. I honestly didn't even realize I had gotten into that rut. Meaning, when the chips are down or I've received a blessing, I'm doing the ping pong thing ...going from pleading to thanking. Back and forth, "I need help. Thank You for Your help. I need help. Thank You for Your help."

Thank you for helping me to be more loving, forgiving, and persistent in the face of hardship, for I can only do all things through You. I don't want to ask for too much. I don't want to be greedy or self serving. God, after all, isn't there to serve me; it needs to be the other way around.

All that being said, it's important to KNOW that when you pray, YOU ARE NOT INCONVENIENCING GOD. God isn't in Heaven saying, "Oh great, it's her again. What's her problem now? She is just never satisfied." We may think like that, but God doesn't think like that! In the Bible it says, "According to your Faith, it will be done unto you."

I have got to get off the "barely getting by" prayers, and move onto the "thanking God ahead of time for bigger things in my life." In other words, I'm going to let my FAITH walk in front of me and start speaking about what God is going to do instead of just speaking about what He's already done.

How do I know that ahead of time? The Bible of course. As Lakewood Church says at every service, "This is my Bible. I am what it says I am. I have what it says I have. I can do what it says I can do."

That's major. Confidence is grounded in Faith. In the name of God, I'm about to do some Huge Things!

My Prayer

Father,

Forgive me for praying like I don't want to trouble You too much. Forgive me for dwelling on my problems and treating them like they are big. Forgive me for the "barely getting by"prayers when I serve a monumental God.

I want to Thank You ahead of time for the flood of favor You are about to unleash on my life this year. Your blessings poured out on me will be my living testament of the Faith I put in front of my problems. I will declare and claim the positive gifts You are about to bestow upon me. You grant swift justice, forgiveness, immeasurable love, above and beyond provision, miraculous healing, and uncontainable happiness to all who have the Faith to make it so.

I believe in all of Your promises. I believe that You never run out. I believe in Your power. I believe that in a split second everything can change just because You decided to make it so. Thank You ahead of time for Your Godly Gifts. Thank You for lining things up behind the scenes to answer my prayers. Thank You for softening hearts, changing attitudes, and giving me the armor of Your words for my own protection and confidence. Thank You for an abundance that I couldn't fathom in my wildest dreams.

I will be bold and act without fear or hesitation because I am Your daughter. I serve You. I want Your will in my life. Your ways are the best ways. Your ways transcend human understanding. I trust You with all that I have and all that I am.

Amen.

Your Worth and Value

Your worth and your value do not come from what you do in life, they come from who you are in God. You do not need to walk around carrying a heavy sack of guilt: Guilt from your past of what you've done or what's been done to you. Guilt from telling others no. Guilt from not being superwoman and being all things to all people. Guilt from feeling like it's wrong NOT to carry some kind of burden every day.

Guilt is no way to live your life. Jesus walked this earth to literally free you from your own guilt by offering you forgiveness. Jesus paid the price for that sack of guilt. He wants you to let that go! Jesus has given you a grand gift! Once you ask for forgiveness, there is no penalty for you to pay.

Never ever ever belittle yourself. You are not a small person who is insignificant in any way. God sees you as AMAZING (after all, you were created in His own image and wouldn't you agree that He is an AMAZING God?!). You have a great future in front of you. Forget about your lousy beginning because God has promised you a great finish!

It's ok to enjoy your life, and it is ok to enjoy yourself. It's ok to just BE HAPPY... You have wonderful things to look forward to. Yield and surrender yourself to your Father — The God of Redemption. Every single day, God's Mercy is renewed. Begin your life anew today! Release your past to Jesus and know that your worth in God's eyes was valuable enough for Him to sacrifice His only Son's life in a most loving way.

I, for one, am embracing a new beginning. I am so very close to ending three very difficult seasons in my life with my health, my job, and a broken relationship (A span of over 16 years of back to back hardship... not even including sporadic hard times prior to that). When Jesus said in the Bible, "It is Finished," that was the beginning of a New Forgiven Life for all of us. I will get to say, "It is Finished" very soon, and I can hardly wait for all my New Seasons to begin! May you all see the excitement that God has planned right in front of you. The "what's next" is thrilling! All God wants from us is to BE who He intended us to be. Anything apart from that will always be a struggle.

God is worth the life you live. Heaven is worth any hardship. You are worth dying for. You are valuable. You are loved. You are forgiven, so release your guilt. Happiness is a deserved feeling that God wants you to have, not just for now, but for an eternity. Pray for people everywhere to discover their self worth in God's eyes.

Value and Worthlessness

When we go to Heaven and stand before Christ, we will approach Him one of two ways...either with confidence, or we will shrink away from Him in shame. Our deeds on earth will be laid bare. The motivations of our heart will be examined. Will we be triumphant or stumble? Did we live a life of self indulgence? Did we live a life full of worthless acts according to God? Or did we live a life of value: leading others to Christ, loving others the way we should, and glorifying God with our behavior?

These are not thoughts to be considered in our final hours. These are thoughts that should be at the forefront of our daily living right now. Living a life of purpose, sharing the gifts that we've been entrusted with, and making the most of the time we have left on earth by serving others and in turn, serving God. Our highest priority should be seeking first the kingdom of God. We should do things that will bear fruit in Heaven not on Earth. Trivial pursuits only end in emptiness.

In our earthly suffering, we learn empathy for others. We are lovingly disciplined to understand what has value and what is worthless in our lives. It changes you and evolves what you choose to pursue. Please consider your endeavors from Christ's perspective, because one day you will have to explain yourself. You know in your heart right from wrong, and nothing escapes the division of your deeds between these two categories: value and worthlessness.

I wouldn't be a good friend if I didn't care about your eternal future. So, know that there is love behind every word I say. May we all be able to walk with confidence, knowing we did what we could, when we could, and put the needs of others before our own.

Jesus' Whole Life

"And I suppose that if all the other events in Jesus' life were written, the whole world could hardly contain the books!"
— John 21:25

Note: Scrambled Eggs. I always say, "Scrambled eggs" when it's a little bit of jumbled up everything. That means the following information comes from historians (not the Bible itself), a little from the Bible, and a little of my own two cents worth. I think the information is on point or I wouldn't write about it, but I still have to say, "Scrambled Eggs."

Can you imagine? We have only caught a glimpse into Jesus' life. We know very little of His younger years. Through historians, we do know where He went to school in Nazareth and the synagogues He attended. Most of His moral training and spiritual culture came from his own home. His parents taught Him right from wrong. In other words....God chose His parents wisely. Apparently, Jesus was extremely smart (imagine that). He knew three languages by the age of seven and could communicate with more people than most. He posed many questions as a youth, searching for (or teaching others) answers.

As He grew, Jesus spent a great deal of time in his father's repair shop and met a huge variety of people traveling in caravans from many different lands. Nazareth was a caravan way station and crossroads of travel. The caravan travelers and conductors gave Jesus perspective on the human condition. He also heard from the world's greatest spiritual thinkers, of the day, when they traveled through Jesus' synagogue. Jesus had the opportunity to really know an expanse of the human race. He thoroughly understood men, and all their difficult life problems, and DEVOTEDLY LOVED THEM. (My favorite written comment about Jesus outside of what's written in the Bible directly).

That's how I feel every day. Devotedly loved by Jesus. How could you not? He gave His own life that we may be free forever. That's not only knowing the human condition of His day...that's knowing the human condition for all time. I look around and think... "Am I the only one blown away by this monumental gift?" I know what real suffering is. I know humility more than I realized was possible. I know the sacrifice of Jesus.

Jesus did amazing, wonderful things in His lifetime that were recorded. Before those written recordings of life events....He lived His whole life in preparation to be the greatest example of a human being we could ever know. He didn't just show up on the scene as a full grown man and say, "Check me out...I can perform miracles. My dad can beat up your dad. I have legions of angels at my command. Don't mess with me." Absurd. Jesus was humble. He never accumulated anything of monetary value. He served others. He healed better than any doctor. You name a moral value...He had it to perfection. Above all, He forgave and loved others, and this very second, HE LOVES YOU!

My Prayer

Thank You for giving me the gift of EVERYTHING. I realize that Your sacrifice opened up the gates of Heaven for me. Accepting You as my Lord and Savior is the best decision I've ever made. I can hardly wait to hug You first when I leave this earth; to be in Your presence and say the words, "I love You. Thank You for allowing me to live in paradise forever." Although I'm not perfect, I wake up every day with my heart in the right place. I will never give up trying to live up to Your example. As You commanded, I will feed Your little lambs. I will reach out to love, teach, and give until You call me home.

Amen. Amen. Amen

Where Do You Keep God?

Yesterday, I listened to someone complain, at length, about an ongoing problem they were having with a family member. To handle the problem they were in counseling and pursuing other ways of "handling it." My first and only question was... "Have you prayed about it?" After a long awkward pause, the answer was yes. I could tell by their reaction that praying was their last resort and God is kept in their pocket...kind of like a trump card. How can I tell? It was unnatural for them to have a conversation including God. God is kept secret.

It begged the question for me...Where do we keep God? Literally, where do we keep Him?

Some keep God in church and close the doors, to keep Him in there for next week. Some keep God on their answering machines, so they can broadcast their allegiance to the King of Kings to anyone who calls. Some keep God in their night stands or under their bed where they keep their Bible, journals or diaries. Some keep God where they keep Santa Claus...in their Christmas cards and Holiday decorations. Some keep God in childhood memories of going to church. Some keep God on the floor....That way He's easy to reach for when they hit rock bottom. Some keep God in their pocket, so no one else can see their secret. Some keep God on their car radios, but they change the station when others need a ride. Some keep God on a very high dusty shelf behind a trophy that they would need a ladder to get to. Some keep God in their Kleenex boxes and only pray when they've been brought to tears.

Where do I keep God? I remembered the very moment I knew I kept God with me everywhere. I was in a movie where I usually go to escape from the reality of life....a movie to entertain me. God kept permeating my thoughts. I thought what if God came down to earth right now and I'm in the movies? Would He be mad that I wasn't out doing better things with my time? Would He approve of my movie selection? Then, I sat in the movies (for the first time ever) and prayed. It became a frequent thing with me. I'm somewhere lost in another world on film, and I'm thinking about God and praying for those sitting next to me and issues that surround my day.

I became aware that I take God with me everywhere – I save Him a seat right beside me. He's with me at volleyball, in traffic, when I'm getting dressed, when I eat, when I'm in bed, when I'm at Duke, when I'm with friends and family... EVERYWHERE.

I hope you have that moment of recognition in your lives. I know that no matter where I am or what I'm doing, He is in my thoughts all day long. It wasn't always that way. I'm not going to lie and say that's the case. But I will say it has evolved over time.

The more I consciously made time for God in my life, the more He was in every part of my life, whether I made the effort or not. He made the effort because He knew my heart belonged to Him. I was seeking Him.

It's a great feeling to be that close to God. It really is. I may not have everything go "my way," but I'm not braving rough waters alone. Never alone.

Where do I keep God? Right next to me and inside of me... everywhere I go and any time of the day or night.

Where do YOU keep God?

Chapter 9

Choose Light

Hi

"Search me, O God, and know my heart; test my thoughts. Point out anything you find in me that makes you sad, and lead me along the path of everlasting life."

— Psalm 139:23-24

Every job, friendship, and romance began with some variation of the word, "Hi."

"Hello, howdy, nice to meet you, my name is so and so — what's yours? Bonjour, hi."

It's so easy to make a connection with another person, and it all starts with a simple introduction. The problem is we isolate ourselves with our iPods, cell phones, books, errands, and shyness (and I firmly believe cell phones are the absolute worst). Frequently, we don't fully engage with someone (that we know) sitting across the table from us, let alone walk up to a person we find interesting just to say, "Hi," and start a conversation.

People crave companionship. We have a great deal to learn from one another that we miss out on by staying in our own private comfort zones! My friends often think I'm this super confident person, and I'm truly not; I have to pray for boldness because it's the only way I'm going to be able to reach out in His name.

Yesterday, I had another long day at Duke, but I finally figured out a way to NOT make it all about me or focus on how bad the chemo is going to make me feel. I came bearing candles, little gifts, notes, flowers, toys for kids, or snacks; these items made it easier for me to start a conversation when I approach people with a thoughtful gesture. They let their guard down with a stranger, and we get to know each other very quickly. Sometimes, we exchange a hug, phone numbers, or email addresses, but the biggest thing we exchange is encouragement and a smile. Man, that makes my day! It feels selfish, in a way, to give, because I'm receiving a massive amount of joy.

You are missing out on the greatest feeling when you keep to yourself...you truly are. I'm not saying that you have to buddy up with everyone in the room and invite people over to your house for dinner, but I am saying to reach out to someone who needs your kind words and smiling face today. When you look up from your devices (computers, iPads, and phones), look around; there's someone who needs you today. They will be easy to spot and noticeable. It may be the mom in the grocery store line looking embarrassed because her kids are throwing a tantrum. It may be the person behind you pumping gas, driving a beat up car, looking dejected because of the price of gas. It may be the waitress that had to work a double shift to support their family. It may be someone who is obviously very sick. Look around...they are everywhere.

Saying, "Hi" with a smile or starting a quick conversation says to another person, "You matter, You are noticeable, You are important, You are cared about." That's what the world needs. You have the ability to give that gift to another person repeatedly throughout your day. Don't hold back. You will open the floodgates of joy in your own life when you master this skill.

I just wanted to extend a great big smile :) and say, "HI! Have a great day! I'm thinking about you. I'm praying for you. You are loved. You matter to me and to God. You are worthy of joy every day."

Chapter 10

You Who Cheerfully Sow

Seasonal Prayers and Callings

"...He who sows sparingly will also reap sparingly, and he who sows bountifully will also reap bountifully. So let each one give as he purposes in his heart, not grudgingly or of necessity; for God loves a cheerful giver. And God is able to make all grace abound toward you..."

— 2 Corinthians 9:6-8

Winter

It never fails. Every year when the weather turns cold, my very first thought turns to those who literally have to sleep outside. My heart hurts when I think about it. It makes my stomach sick. The start of winter brings me to my knees to pray gratitude prayers...Thank You God that I have a home, blankets, warm food, a comfortable bed, and heat. I feel called to go through my closets and donate whatever I can to those that don't have what I have. Am I really using every coat, sweater, and blanket, or would it serve someone else better?

When I could drive, I would go around just looking for people on the side of the road that looked forgotten, so I could help them in some small way. (A pair of gloves, a meal, a sleeping bag, a Bible... something)

Spring

Spring means opening the windows and letting the fresh air in. It's the time of rebirth and flowers blooming everywhere. It's also spring cleaning time - removing the clutter. With my cancer, I've constantly been removing the clutter from my life, cleaning out every drawer, every cabinet, under the beds, every closet, and an impossibly big attic. Simplifying. We keep a tremendous amount of things that we don't need, and we still go out to buy more and more and more. The closer I get to the end of my life, the more I want less and less and less. Contentment and freedom comes with less...I know... crazy right? I feel this pull to give most of what I've spent a lifetime accumulating all away. It feels really good to lighten the load. I pray that God points out to me who would like to receive the things I want to let go of.

Summer

Heat and humidity. I think God created the ocean so we could escape the southern summer temperatures. I look at that huge body of water, and I'm in awe of it: the countless creatures that lie beneath its surface in their own ecosystem, the fact that tiny grains of sand hold it back from covering the entire planet. I even think about how God literally split it in two for Moses. Can you even imagine being there to see that? We sit on back porches and docks to watch magnificent sunsets that change nightly. Some days, we experience fierce afternoon thunderstorms with pounding rain and ominous clouds. I'm impressed with God's creation. Nature blows me away. I'm reminded of His power and His gentle beauty. I'm reminded of how important it is that we take care of our planet...that we do our part to contribute to its longevity. I pray God helps me to encourage others to recycle, etc.

Fall

My favorite time of year. I think of long walks and warm coffee or hot chocolate. I think of cooking and baking. I want to have people over to share in a meal. My thoughts turn to those who don't know where their next meal is coming from. I skipped a few meals in my day when I was "too busy to eat" with long work hours. I never missed meals because I didn't have the money or resources. There are many children in our community that literally miss meals every day and don't know when they will eat again: a fear of no food, their stomachs rumbling out of starvation. I think about them and about the child in Africa we sponsor that used to eat old leftover food from a trash dump. How can I eat these big meals and stuff myself knowing full well that families are going hungry? I want to donate to the local soup kitchen. After taking a tour, I learned that they are overcome with donations over the holidays and have to skimp in the dead of winter and heat of summer, so I write in my calendar to help them when they need it the most. Not a single Thanksgiving goes by that I'm not humbled by God's generous provision for my family. The calling then becomes to provide for those who don't have equal provision. To whom much has been given...much is expected.

I write all these things, not to have the "me show," but to get you to think about what the change in seasons means to you. What do you pray for, and how does God call you to serve during that season? Think about it.

> *"And let us not grow weary of doing good, for in due season we will reap, if we do not give up."*
> — Galatians 6:9

Your Power To Do Good

"Do not withhold good from those to whom it is due, when it is in your power to do it."

— Proverbs 3:27

I read that this morning and thought, "Wow!" If that doesn't pull at your heart to pitch in and help someone, I don't know what does. How many times a day do we withhold good from those who deserve it? I'm going to venture out and say probably more often than we think. Some examples to think about:

1. We eat three meals a day knowing there are people in our own town who have gone days without food. I think we get by with doing this because we don't have to look them in the face every day. Think you don't have the power to change that? Try skipping a meal once or twice a week and put the money you would have spent on that meal in a jar. At the end of the year, take that money and go to any food donation drop off and either drop off the money or better yet... buy the food they need the most and drop it off. Better still...serve that food and look into someone's grateful eyes. Then, you can see the magnitude of your very small sacrifice. Have more to give? Give it.

2. I can guarantee you there are a ton of very lonely people suffering from sickness or abandoned by their families in nursing homes. Don't have a single day where you are bored? Don't even have one hour ever to spare? Your time would be precious to someone who is all alone. Play a hand of cards, read them a book, bring them some flowers, or write an encouraging card. What, Teresa!? That's crazy... I'm a stranger to them. My response is, "Who cares?" I'm a stranger to every single person I meet at Duke every time I go. It never fails. I watch their disposition change to happiness in the smallest amount of time spent with them. Sometimes, people just want a listening ear to tell you their story. Unless your ears are missing, I'm pretty sure you are capable of doing that.

3. Yesterday, I had four people come to my house and do a long list of things for me. They brought me tons of food,

hung Christmas Lights out in the cold weather, assembled and fixed things in my house, ran errands for me at several different places, and plan on coming back to plant flowers in my yard and deliver groceries. For a cancer patient who can't be out in the elements or exposed to too many germs out in public, that is a big fat giant prayer answered and then some! Do you not know of a single person who could benefit from rolling your sleeves up and pitching in? Is someone you know moving and could use an extra set of hands? Does someone you know have the flu and could use your help picking up their kids from school? Can you transport someone to get their car fixed? How about pulling your neighbor's trash can in for them? How about giving a stranger your great parking space because they are older than you or have small children, even though you were there first?

In case it needs pointing out....
1 = money
2 = time
3 = effort

In large or small quantities, you have the power and ability to do good things. Opportunity is literally all around you. Don't withhold that gift from others. You not only cheat them, you cheat yourself.

Giving

"When a friend is in trouble, don't annoy him by asking if there is anything you can do. Think up something appropriate and do it."

— E.W. Howe

"For if you give, you will get! Your gift will return to you in full and overflowing measure, pressed down, shaken together to make room for more, and running over. Whatever measure you use to give-large or small-will be used to measure what is given back to you."

— Luke 6:38

"Do not withhold good from those who deserve it when it's in your power to help them."

— Proverbs 3:27

I could list hundreds of quotes about giving. For some reason, as we drift away from Thanksgiving and Christmas.... we gradually slip into "me" mode. It's easy to come up with countless excuses of why we can't help someone else. Every single excuse we have is generally rooted in the "me" category. I could use the excuse that I have cancer, and I'm quarantined because of germs. That's not even a good excuse. My hand isn't broken. I have money in the bank. I own stamps. I can write a check to St. Jude's to help children with cancer. Not out of obligation...but out of love. I may not be able to venture out and socialize in the world right now, but I can write emails and spread God's word that way. I can do kind things for other patients at Duke when I am there. I know what it feels like to be a patient.

I have been on the receiving end of some much needed giving, and I couldn't be more grateful. I have also been forgotten several times when I was dependent on someone's offer for help. I've also heard every excuse in the book from those who felt guilty for not helping me. We all live with our choices in life. Eventually, all those choices will be laid out in front of

God. I'm pretty sure He isn't going to buy a bunch of excuses. Our actions speak for themselves. I'm not trying to convict anyone. I'm just reminding all of us (including myself) to give from a place of love and not guilt. That is the kind of giving that fills your heart with joy. Giving should never be a checklist item in your day.

My greatest joys in life have always been when I've given someone else a labor of love. My time is more precious to me now than it has ever been. I wouldn't take back my time from a single party or wedding that I've done over the years. Each one was a gift of love from me to a client (most of whom I became friends with).

I long to give. It makes me so happy to wrap a present and surprise someone I care about. I love writing cards to express my appreciation and love for all the unselfish, giving people in my life. I hope that you can all give to someone in need with a loving, kind heart and never out of a sense of obligation. It is a gift you will get back in equal measure!

God's Gift of Overcoming the World

A miracle is something that seems impossible and happens anyway. It's a surprising Gift from God. It's been a crazy week. The world has given me many: "Awwwwww, too bad for you moments," every time, God has answered with: "Check out the gifts I have for you."

Here are some examples from my life this week:

- The world: Oh, the weather outside is frightful from here to there! We had very bad driving conditions with sections of white out snow and ice from Wilmington to Duke. It took us five hours (even driving three mph at times) to drive a distance that normally takes us less than half that time.

- God's gift: In a sea of car wrecks and stalled cars, I delivered you without a scratch!

- The world: You can't go home today because the valet lost your car and your car keys for over an hour, and the roads are too dangerous because you got done too late with your doctor appointments. The governor declared a state of emergency. You packed nothing and are totally unprepared to stay.

- God's gift: I have a nice nurse who will give you free t-shirts to sleep in. The valet supervisor will give you several free parking passes to use in the future. I have a manager at a nice hotel waiting to give you toiletries and a plush room because of your story today. She will give you double the room size, double the bed sizes, an extra bathroom, and a living room, less than half the cost, a great view, and extended stay for three nights. I have your niece ready to bring you the best chicken wrap you've ever eaten in your life, and you will have a wonderful evening of heartfelt conversation. You will grow in your love and understanding of each other.

- The world: You can't see your son for three days unexpectedly.

- God's gift: I have a neighbor ready to step in and help you by taking care of your son as if he were her own. You will be greeted by your son, when you return, with the biggest hug and gratitude for all you do for him every day.

- The world: After changing all your plans to stay near the cancer center to get chemo and a scary taxi ride in eight inches of snow, you will arrive at an empty ghost town and be greeted with the words, "Nobody called you? We are closed. Everyone is going home. There is no chemo at Duke today."

- God's gift: After going upstairs to see for myself, I ran into the pharmacy administrator with her coat on to head home. We began talking. I told her how important it was for me to get chemo today. She called my doctor, and he told her to personally mix my chemo and to call a nurse in to administer it today!!!! And yes, that's just what happened! The world said no, but God said, "Yes!" She called so many nurses that they had enough for a whole staff, and other patients who trickled in got their chemo too. We had no food because the cafeterias were closed. So, we ordered pizzas and ate fundraiser candy! All were a gift from Duke for our inconvenience (but really a gift from God).

- The world: You were the first ones in and the very last ones to leave the cancer center. It was dark and hard to tell if the roads would become all ice too quickly. Your car was buried in a blanket of snow, in the hotel parking lot, that had to be dug out.

- God's gift: Six people laughed and scraped heaping piles of snow off my car (complete strangers joined in on the fun using scrapers and brooms, when they saw us using our bare hands). Afterwards, we made a run for it and found out the roads were not icy. It was as if God cleared a path for us because traffic was nowhere to be found. Several times we were either alone on the road or saw one or two cars in the far distance. Our car had wings, and we made great time.

Time and time again people went out of their way to help me. What an enormous gift from God. The world put up roadblock after roadblock, and God lined up the right people, the right circumstances, and the right times for me to have not only solutions but something better.

Try not to get discouraged by what the world gives you, because God has many gifts He wants to give you to make your life better. Look for them. Thank God and choose to be a light for others: Pay it forward!

> *"I have told you these things, so that in me you may have peace. In this world you may have trouble. But take heart! I have overcome the world."*
>
> — John 16:33

A Prayer for Hard Times

God,

Pour the grace of hope upon me, and allow me always to see the light of hope burning brightly in front of me.

Light up the darkness by filling me with faith and hope and allowing me to receive the comfort of Your love.
Give me the courage and strength to know that I will get through these hard times.

Fill me with the joy and trust of knowing that I am your child and that You will care for me and those I love.

Hear my prayer,

Amen

Chapter 11

Give Your Days to Him

Starting Your Day Off Right

"O righteous Father! The world has not known You, but I have known You; and these have known that You sent Me. And I have declared to them Your name, and will declare it, that the love with which You loved Me may be in them, and I in them."

— John 17:25-26

Every morning we all have our routines. Some of us didn't sleep well the night before because of worry. Some of us are behind before we even step foot out of bed. Some of us can't open our eyes before that first cup of coffee.

BEFORE you go to your job, take your trip, feed the family, make your to do lists, and plan your day...start it off right.

The best thing you can do for yourself is cast ALL your cares and worries on The Lord because He is waiting for you to give them to Him.

"Can anyone of you by worrying add a single hour to your life?"

— Matthew 6:27

"Commit to The Lord whatever you do, and he will establish your plans."

— Proverbs 16:3

"Cast your cares on The Lord and he will sustain you; he will never let the righteous be shaken."

— Psalm 55:22

My Prayer

Lord, I want to cast my cares on You today. It is not my job to fix everything, change anyone, or let my worries steal away my precious time. I will let You establish my plans, so I can start my day off the right way.

I will lift up every concern that troubles my heart and lay them out before You; for what You can do in the blink of an eye, takes me so much longer. I also realize that some of the things on my plate today are just work lists that I created myself and not necessities. Help me prioritize and remember what's truly important.

Help me to take a deep breath in the silence of Your presence, and know peace instead of chaos. Help me to shrink the things I dread so that I can handle them in small bites. Take away all my fears and replace them with Your confidence and strength. Keep reminding me that I have not, because I ask not.

I'm asking You this morning to step into my entire day, so I can replay this passage in my head over and over again:

"This is the day that The Lord has made.
I will rejoice and be glad in it."

A GIANT AMEN!

How to Start Your Day When You Are in a Hole

"Then Jesus said, "Did I not tell you that if you believe, you will see the glory of God?"

— John 11:40

"I pray that God, the source of hope, will fill you completely with joy and peace because you trust in Him. Then you overflow with confident Hope through the power of the Holy Spirit."

— Romans 15:13

Guess who believes regardless of how bad I feel right now? Guess who believes regardless of what my day was like yesterday? Guess who believes I can be healed even though I know cancer has a firm grip on my bones? Guess who believes when my circumstances don't look great for the next month? Guess who believes even though I woke up in terrible back pain every 30 minutes last night. This girl right here!!! If I was in a crowd of thousands, of other terminally ill cancer patients, I would stand up and say, "I still believe. God has nothing to prove to me. My life can be turned around in an instant. I know it can."

I don't care how deep the hole is that you are in right now (trust me when I say...mine's pretty deep). God's reach has no limit. I'm going to start this new day repeating the word of God. When I hurt, I will remember all the times God delivered me in the past. I will remember every miracle, big and small, in my life for He is greater than the cancer inside of me. He doesn't need a shovel to dig me out. I'm reminded of the day I shaved my head before chemo, and I couldn't feel sadness after my prayer. That day, I prayed for God to pull me up higher than Satan was pulling me down.

My Prayer

Father, I'm starting in the hole today. My skin is burning, my bones are aching, and my nerves are pulling in every direction

119

towards pain. Satan would love to keep me laying on my back, in this pit of despair, but I'm not messing around. I don't want to stay here. I need You today to pull me up. I'm dependent on Your power, because I am too weak on my own. As the sun comes up and sheds light on a dark world, fill my morning with Your light. I trust Your long term plan for me, because I believe You love me more than I could ever love myself. Hold my hand, and I will keep my eyes upon You, and not around me.

Thank You that yesterday doesn't have to be my today, because I BELIEVE... I HAVE CONFIDENT HOPE IN YOU.

Amen.

Closeness to God

You are the closest to God when you are living out His purpose for your life. When you are helping those in need, when you are loving others, when you are seeking His will and living in His word, He is right there! You can feel His presence deep in your soul when you are doing the things you know please Him most. Those times when you feel broken-hearted, alone, lost, and discouraged are the easiest times to speak to Him in humbleness and without other distractions. When you are sick and isolated in bed, He is closely watching over you.

The question of distance from God is our doing – not His. Our distractions from Him include: technology (I think this one is huge!), careers (it's amazing how much of our time work takes from us), other relationships (how many friends and family pull you in different directions?), money (it's very tempting to spend money on so many non-essential things), and basically anything that we desire for ourselves and not for the good of mankind. I will be the first to say that I fall short on so many levels. It actually makes me ashamed that I give into such a variety of distractions daily. Sadly, I'm just short changing myself when I do that.

I never want to live a day without feeling the presence of God close to me. I can honestly say, when you seek Him with all your heart, He will reveal Himself in huge miraculous ways. We are not talking about a creator that lives on a distant planet where we have to travel far just to see Him. We are talking about a Father that wants to be right next to us ALL THE TIME. You either include God or exclude God. What percentage of time do you give to Him? He gives you 100% of His. My desire is to find new ways to include and integrate Him into my entire day and not fragments or pieces of it. The ways of the world grow dim and bleak in comparison to the truthful light of His ways.

"As the Heavens are higher than the Earth, so are my ways higher than your ways."

My Prayer

Father, take me to new heights as I seek to spend more time with You. I realize that I've let distractions separate us at times, and I ask You to forgive me for distancing myself from You. I know that You desire me to be close— I want that too. I will look at the world through the eyes of Your Son. Grant me the resolve to walk the right paths and make better choices. It feels good to be near You. It feels like the warm sun on my skin when I sit on the beach. It's comforting and peaceful.

You fill me with bold confidence to step out in faith. You make me want to be a better person. You give me a deeper understanding of what heaven on earth looks like. You have poured out an abundance of spiritual knowledge that I soak up like a sponge. You show me things that I once turned a blind eye to before.

Thank You for shedding a brilliant light on the things that please You most. I love Your ways, and I eternally love You.

Amen!

God Created Us Different

I'm going to tell on myself and put me on top of the guilty list this morning. This weekend, I found myself getting very irritated with numerous people, who in my mind, just weren't towing the line. They were being lazy, unaccountable, complacent, and in my eyes... they just fell short of my expectation of them. Now here's where it gets brutally honest. I couldn't let it go. My temper (that I haven't seen in quite awhile) was just brewing and boiling over to the point that I had to just let it out. I feel better right now even confessing it to you via email, blog, and book (it's not good to bottle stuff up). I literally told someone that their workers needed to be fired!

This is the part where I need to keep myself in Christian check. I told someone I better check myself before I wreck myself. Now, I'm back in God's Word today and reflecting on my interactions with others. Let's just say that I felt convicted by what I read: "We will receive from God in the same measure what we give to others." For me, tolerance, forgiveness, understanding, and perspective were all off the table this past weekend. I looked at things only through my eyes, and why weren't they behaving the way I would? That answer is simple: "God created us all to be different."

Don't get me wrong...I'm not planning on condoning unacceptable behavior just to be "excused and accepted" to the point that the others I meet feel like they can just repeatedly have this "not my responsibility" kind of attitude. What I'm saying is that I am in charge of ME and how I'm reflecting Christ with my own behavior regardless of what others do or don't do.

Was I a blessing to them in my anger? Doubt it. Could I stand before God and say I exercised patience, forgiveness, and understanding to my fellow man? Nope! Did they see my love for Christ in my words and actions? Absolutely Not. As I read my own words today, I think to myself, "I better make a change right now." If God were to come down to lift up those that belong to Him this past weekend, I couldn't exactly say, "Could you wait until I'm ready and on my best behavior?"

So, here I am on Sunday — the day of rest and preparation for the week ahead — recognizing my mistakes and screwing my head and heart back in place to be aligned with God. Starting fresh. I realize that not everyone in the world has my standards, but I want to lead someone to the threshold of Jesus' door and not slam it in their face. We can choose our friends, but oftentimes we can't choose our coworkers, fellow committee volunteers, or people that perform a service for us. I did, however, choose God, and with that comes His expectation of how I show my love for Him through MY behavior. Pray for me because, as you know, I'm the girl that sets a pretty high bar for those around me.

Thanks for putting up with me when I'm not "wearing my Sunday best" because apparently, I don't even live up to my own Christian expectations of myself, but I'm working on it.

Choosing Happiness

Abraham Lincoln said, "Most people are as happy as they've decided to be." He also said, "In the end, it's not the years in your life that count... It's the life in your years."

Even with all my health issues, long work hours, and life without a man to share it with, I'm glad I'm me. I look around at how other people CHOOSE to live their lives and think to myself (I'm so glad I'm not you). We should all have the mindset of ownership of our own lives. Meaning, this is the life God has given me, and I plan on making the most of it.

The gift of spiritual sight I've been given by God is an honor. I see people down to their innermost core. What I see the most frequently is unresolved pain, sadness, and bitterness. Unfortunately, most people don't even realize they are holding on to the very cinder block that is causing them to drown. Instead of going to the effort and struggle to carry that weight, they should just let go - releasing their weight so they can come back up out of the water for air.

I recently had two people speak to me in a very rude, condescending, and overly aggressive tone. They weren't mad at me, but instead they were mad about their life choices and decided to take it out on me. Does it sting a little when someone does that to you? Of course it does. Should it be acceptable and tolerated? No, not really...However, we need to quit looking at the surface of other people's behavior and realize there are much deeper issues going on. Aren't you glad you are not them?

As women, our first response is typically an emotional one. We are fragile creatures in an abrasive world. Don't let the unhappiness of others steal your innate JOY. Step back and realize that God will handle that other person in His way and in His time. That's not our job, and our mission in life is not to "fix" other people. We can address their unacceptable behavior and then decide who is going to carry that unhappy cinder block home with them. To tell you the truth, I'm tired of carrying mine, but the other guy, nine times out of ten, will wrap a rope around it and tie it to his leg even tighter, unwilling to let it go – ever.

I choose happiness. I choose to let go of things that weigh me down. I choose to move on. I choose to reach for God when I'm being pulled away from Him. I choose to surround myself with good people. I choose to not let my circumstances influence my decision to enjoy the life that God has given me as a gift. I choose a future that I want to be in wholeheartedly. I choose a smile over tears, a hopeful heart over heartache, a change versus a walk in quicksand, and to not let my final day on earth be about someone else's problems.

I, more than anybody else, know that this day could be my last day here. So, how do I want to spend it? I want to spend it with a smile on my face. I want to spend it being HAPPY!

My Prayer

Father God,

I ask that You help us to not get lost. We lose our way sometimes and don't realize how we got to a place of unhappiness. Sometimes, we make bad choices that cause ourselves pain and suffering. Sometimes, we react to others too quickly and defensively. Sometimes, we feel the need to control everything. Sometimes, we forget that Satan is alive and well, and that other people need rescuing. Sometimes, we are too tired and stressed to cope. Sometimes, we need to step away and ask You to intervene on our behalf.

Thank You for the freedom of choice and the wisdom to choose wisely. Thank You that being Your child entitles us to a heavenly home where happiness is a permanent fixture. Bless these people today and grace their face with a smile, because they chose You to be the source of all their happiest moments.

Amen.

Quality of Life

I'm a firm believer in quality over quantity; it's reflected in everything I do. Yesterday, after going to a funeral, I went and played volleyball for the first time in a year; and yes, I did not have the green light from my doctor. Please save the lectures, because you are talking to a girl who would sneak in the parking lot with my volleyball partner and pepper (hitting a volleyball back and forth to warm up before a game) right before my surgeries at Duke. I even did it left handed when my right side hurt too badly.

You see, volleyball is my greatest passion… it got me through years of pain and suffering after my broken neck. It has always been my great motivator… They told me I would probably never play again, and I felt a wave rush through my body and literally crush my spirit. I went on not only to play but to win some very big tournaments with crowds rooting for the underdog. When they told me I shouldn't play because my bones are so fragile, well frankly, it crushed my spirit a second time. But yesterday, I felt alive again. There's no other way to describe it. I felt like I could play all day (although I didn't go all out and dive like I normally would do, but the rush of playing was still there for me). I actually won three games out of four rotating partners with two on my side against three on the other all while using a men's net. I think I still got it!

My inspiration to play? The man who told his sons on his deathbed, "You are all good sons." It may seem like a simple thing, but it was enough to give all of them closure which is something not many people get.

I would call that a good day to die. What a way to go… surrounded by those you love, getting in your last hugs and compliments. When I broke my neck, before my son was born, that would have been a great day for me to die. It was a holiday (July 4th weekend – my second birthday and also when I got diagnosed with cancer on my third birthday) and the sun was shining. I was tan, and I was out water skiing with family... It wouldn't have been a bad way to go.

If I break every single bone in my body, I would at least be doing it while playing my passion. I can't let go of something I love so much, that I've played since the sixth grade. Quite honestly, I think it would help me get physically fit again: the way I was right before cancer. I know I can't turn back time, but I know who can. So today, I'm going to play. I think I've earned some sunny days at the beach. Yes, I will tell my Doctor, but I'm going to play until they carry me off that court on a stretcher. That's my quality of life.

Yesterday, I cried and mourned, and then I was the happiest I've been in a really long time. Please pray that God will heal me inside out, and hopefully I will use this as inspiration for those who have given up hope (because I got mine back yesterday, and it took somebody who wasn't even on this earth anymore to give it to me). I don't want to be a cancer victim anymore, I will be a victor: Tell God to watch over me when I play as I glorify Him with this endeavor.

Chapter 12

Reflect His Light

Don't Keep Count of Wrongdoings

"I have declared my ways, and You answered me; Teach me Your statutes. Make me understand the way of Your precepts; So shall I meditate on Your wonderful works."

— Psalm 119:26–27

In the Bible, LOVE is described in Corinthians as not keeping record of another's wrong doings.

I've not had an easy time of this. I've had many many people who I thought loved me, and yet, they treated me cruelly. The worst is when they would say something flippantly and unapologetically that stabbed a hole in my heart. Has that ever happened to you? A friend? A family member? A spouse? Someone you've known for decades? I think to myself....why? When did I let you down? When did I make you not feel loved? Why are you so mean to me? I've been nothing but good to you. The answer to all of those questions is: they are retaliating for someone else's behavior in their life. It's easier to face you than them. It's easier to throw you under the bus than look in the mirror. It's easier to express their rage and not hold it in (around those who will stick around and take it). So, once

I know they are capable of hurting me, do I cut them out of my life? Do I sit down and take it?

God tells me to not keep count. God tells me to love the unlovable. God tells me to forgive. I'm going to be real with you and tell you that I'm not very good at that. It hurts. For every minute I've cried about their behavior, they have laughed in equal proportion. How do I not whip out a calculator at that point and add up all their digs, insults, and neglect? The truth is... if Jesus kept piling up the times I've disappointed Him, I would be in eternal trouble. He Loves me. He doesn't keep a record when we ask for forgiveness. As a matter of fact, His life on earth was dedicated to erasing my record and wiping it clean.

There comes a day when you have to decide that you know the definition of Love and want to abide by it, regardless of all the meanies out there. The only way I can is to get Jesus involved in the situation. Jesus can change hearts (yours and theirs). I might not put them at the top of my invitation lists, but I also won't roll my eyes when their name comes up. To be honest, it feels super good not to let hatred dominate more of your thoughts than love. It's a win win for you and a sad place of entrapment for them. Pray for their souls because that is Love the way God intended.

I am grateful that God has infused my life with friends far better than I even deserve. I think of them when I'm tempted to complain. It's way more fun to boast about how kind, wonderful, amazing, and loving they are instead of how awful someone else is.

How Do I Show My Love?

How Do I Show My Love?

This morning, I asked myself not WHO I love, but specifically, HOW do I show my love?

How do I love the planet? I recycle, and I don't litter.

How do I love my son? I teach him right from wrong, provide for him, encourage him, and tell him how special he is to me.

How do I love my friends? I treat them the way I would want to be treated.

How do I love my family? I respect their privacy, I'm loyal and supportive beyond measure, and I make them my biggest priority.

How do I love myself? At times, I don't love myself like I should, but when I do, I take care of my body (which right now is very difficult). I feed my soul with God's Word, I read to continue learning and grow my mind, and I socialize with friends and family to increase my happiness.

How do I love God? I follow the example of His Son, and when I fail, I ask for forgiveness and never give up trying to do what pleases Him.

But, how do I love my enemies?

This is the hardest one. I can easily answer the others because they are EASY to love. I'm convinced that this question is actually extremely important to answer if we ever want to have peace on earth. I love my enemies by praying for them... that's it for me right now. I get frustrated, impatient, angry, and resentful when I'm around my enemies or speak of them.

That has got to change. It just has to. It's my biggest work in progress. Satan wins the battle of hate if I can't figure out how to love my enemies. It is naive to expect them to change, so they are easier to love. I have to take the first step towards love.

Maybe a better question would be, "How SHOULD I love my enemies?" Right now, this is what I can come up with from the top of my head:

Amplify their best quality and minimize their worst.

DO NOT let their name and actions cross my lips to others; it's just a reminder of dislike.

Distance myself from engaging in detrimental interactions with them.

Try understanding where their behavior originates from.

And yes, pray...a lot!

My Prayer

> *Lord,*
>
> *Let there be peace on earth, and let it begin with me. Teach me how to love because Your ways are better than my ways.*
>
> Amen.

Kindness Big and Small

Why do people do kind things for strangers? Out of the goodness of their heart is the common answer. I say that goodness comes from God...a whisper in your ear to help them. They need you, and if you don't help, maybe no one else will.

Yesterday, I left my umbrella in the waiting room in the cancer center. After I was done with my appointment, the lady who had been sitting next to me got up and brought it to me when she saw me leaving. A small gesture? Big if I was stuck in a downpour outside. I had to park on the upper parking deck outside and was the furthest car away on a rainy day.

On the drive home, I saw an elderly man with car trouble by the side of the road. Unfortunately, it was on a busy four lane highway during rush hour, and it would be hard for anyone to stop and help him. He probably has a cell phone. If not, someone else has probably already called a tow truck for him, or maybe he has AAA (Triple A). But what if everyone else had those same thoughts and none of that is true? He would be stranded with everyone believing that someone else was helping him. So, I called to get the highway patrol out there to help him. A small gesture? Maybe, but it could be big if he had to wait for hours for help to finally arrive (and on a hot day too).

I watch people all the time in public. Do you open doors for people and let them in first? Do you let the mom with the cranky kids ahead of you in line? Do you let the lady with the tag showing on her dress know? Do you encourage a sales clerk, cashier, or waitress when you can tell they are just having a really stressful day? When traffic is bad, do you let that person come in off a side street? Nobody will know if you help that stranger or not, but you... right? Wrong. The world is watching... I'm watching... God is watching. When you do kind things, it is contagious. Kids pay attention to what they are shown. As grown ups, we can become jaded and think, "I don't have time. I'm in a hurry." Really? Are we ever too busy to be kind to a stranger? God's never been "too busy" to help us.

Back to kindness being big or small, I think there is no such thing as a small kindness. Any time we reach out and unselfishly help someone else, that kindness is always BIG. It also has a way of growing bigger because it causes a chain reaction. Some people refer to that chain reaction as paying it forward. It's easier to be kind to our family and friends since we know them and we treasure them. Today, I encourage you to be kind to strangers. Nothing is too small.

My Prayer

Father God, help us to see strangers as a part of our own family. Make us more aware of how we can be an extension of the kindness and mercy that You have shown us. I know sometimes we get so caught up in our daily lives that we become numb to the larger world around us, within arms reach. We sometimes overlook the little gestures that could make our world a better place. Help us see that the small picture influences the big picture...and it starts with us. Every day, in every way, help us love as we are loved.

Amen.

What Do You Say?

Several times, I have had friends and relatives just kind of disappear on me when I get really bad news, because they are at a loss for words and just don't know what to say to me. Oftentimes, they have lost someone they love to a similar disease, and they put that loved one's face on me. I am already in an isolated prison because of cancer. There is nothing worse than being left completely alone. So, I'm giving this advice not only from my perspective, but to hopefully help you know how to talk to anyone who is hurting.

What do you say?

"I love you."

"I wish I could take this burden away from you."

Comforting words are anything from the Bible that are God's promises.

"Just know that when I'm not physically there to hold your hand, I'm with you in thought and spirit."

Share a memory or laughable moment. Yes, laughing is better than crying. Funny cards are appropriate (somber is not what people need when they are sad). Keep me up to date on your day to day living (just because I'm not out in the world doesn't mean I don't want to hear about it... as a matter of fact, I crave to hear about life as usual for you... it gives me a piece of "normalcy"). Talk about future plans... especially travel (I can't travel, but I can live vicariously through you). Pictures are always great! I see sad faces all the time... it's a relief to see happy faces!

Lastly, cancer is not who I am. It's an unwelcome guest in my life that I didn't ask to visit. It gains power if it separates you from me. If it takes away my loved ones, it wins. I'm still the same me I've always been. I just don't look the same, and I'm sick inside. I still laugh at the same things. I still love working puzzles. I'm still passionate about art, design, and beauty (especially flowers and fixing up my home). I still have a heart for charitable endeavors. I still love movies and music! I still love cooking and baking. I'm happiest at Christmas. In other words, cancer hasn't changed my personality, it just makes me cry sometimes, and I could use a pick me up now and then.

What do you say? Say anything... just don't disappear on me.

I thank God for the people He keeps in my life. They are my angels without wings. Marilyn Monroe said, "If you can't handle me at my worst, you certainly don't deserve me at my best." I'm going to have some worst moments... but first chance I get, I'm going to have some best ones too.

Private Sanctuary

There are very few places that are truly quiet enough to hear your own breathing. My favorite place to write you these emails is early in the morning at my kitchen counter sitting on a bar stool drinking a fresh cup of coffee with the gentle hum of the refrigerator in the background. It's still. It's quiet. It's comfortable. It's become part of my morning routine. The day doesn't feel right to me without it. I sit and reflect on yesterday, today, and tomorrow. I read my devotional and/ or Bible and think about how the words have impacted me or maybe what I could be improving on.

It occurred to me this morning that in the past, I never took my "quiet time" to the deepest level I could. If I was in bed praying or thinking about God in the car or taking a walk on the beach by myself, wasn't that enough? Actually, that's great, but THE NEXT STEP is even better.

We all need a PRIVATE SANCTUARY, a place to go, to be alone without distractions. It should be comfortable, quiet, peaceful, relaxing. A place where you can hear your own breathing, a place where you won't be interrupted. I drive down to the beach now close to sunset, as most of the people are gone around that time. I walk to an area where I can just sit and look out at the vast endless ocean. Your senses become sharper when they aren't processing too many things at once. My brain is working at 100%. I can think clearly. Pray clearly. Listen clearly. It's my own private place. At home, it's my kitchen barstool in the morning or my back steps in the evening.

Do you have a private sanctuary? If you don't, find one. If you do, USE IT! If you use it every day, you will find your soul nourished, refueled – you will feel more peaceful, happier. This isn't a maybe kind of thing. I guarantee it. Give the gift of quiet time to yourself...to God. Make it part of your routine, not when it's convenient. If you wait until you have extra time to make that happen, how's that been working out for you so far? If you already have been diligent about doing so, changes of scenery can breathe new life into your quiet time. Go explore some other places. I'm just giving you a gentle nudge.

LUMI (love u mean it)!

Count Your Blessings

God has a way of showing me things when I start to get down on myself. You see, I feel a little cheated sometimes when it comes to lost time. I will never get back the years I lost in bad relationships or time spent in the hospital and at home recovering from 13 surgeries. That time is gone, and occasionally, I miss it.

This past weekend, I came across these things...

I read about a man who had to get a face transplant, because he was so badly burned that he lost his eyes, mouth, and nose.

I saw a TV show about a military man who only had one partial arm and no legs, because he lost his limbs fighting for our freedom.

I saw an elderly man walking the beach. He was clearly struggling to walk normally.

Lastly, I still think about that little girl at Duke with her head shaved, a huge scar across her skull, hooked up to a breathing machine, and being wheeled down the hallway with parents in tears close behind. She looked at me and smiled. She smiled. I will never forget that little girl.

So, for all you people feeling the Monday blahs...count your blessings. Your problems aren't as big as you think. There will always be someone out there that has it far worse than you. If they can find a way to be happy in the midst of their circumstances, so can you. Look at what you *have* and not at what you've *lost*. Count your blessings — there are many.

"Because The Lord is my Shepherd, I have everything I need!"
— Psalm 23:1

141

What Holds Your Heart?

Plant a Seed

"For where your treasure is, there your heart will be also."
— Matthew 6:21

Every morning when I drop my son off at school, my usual parting words are "Have a great day...I love you...plant some good seeds!"

Planting a seed is helping someone grow into Greatness through your actions or words. You can invest in their future by a compliment, believing in them when no one else does, inspiring them, sharing your knowledge, giving more than you take from them, and above all, loving them for who they are.

Where do you plant a seed? Look around, I'm sure you will see many people that could use one. All it takes is one person to believe in you, to speak a kind word to you, to inspire you, and it changes your life forever. Wouldn't you love to be that person in someone else's life?

When I was in the Third Grade, my art teacher encouraged me to enter a poster contest. I wasn't even into art at the time. I went on to win the contest and become the state youth ambassador for the American Lung Association. I was in commercials, my poster was the Easter Seal for that year, and it was printed on scarves and stamps. I received a beautiful plaque, I rode on parade floats, I was featured in several newspapers, I met people in government with a tour of the White House, I met the whole Duke basketball team and got a signed ball, I met Santa Claus (like the one in Miracle on 34th Street), and I even met people from Sesame Street and got a signed picture (pretty cool when you're a kid).

All of this because one person saw something in me that nobody else did. Beyond my youth, I have pursued the artistic side of myself, and that list of achievements is huge. What if that teacher hadn't encouraged me? What if she never planted that seed in me?

I've had people tell me later that something I said to them had a monumental impact on their life. I had no idea it was that important to them. What if I had remained silent that day?

You just never know how big that seed you plant can grow. Plant the seed. Help someone reach their full potential by your words and actions. It's a really good feeling to be a spark that ignites a flame!

Enjoy your weekend and be on the lookout for opportunities — they are all around you!

Bearing Fruit

"But blessed is the one who trusts in The Lord, whose confidence is in Him. They will be like a tree planted by the water that sends out it's roots by the stream. It does not fear when heat comes; it's leaves are always green. It has no worries in a year of drought and never fails to bear fruit."

— Jeremiah 17:7-8

I want to be that tree! I want to always bear fruit! I may have heat and drought trying to attack me, but my roots run deep. I drink from the stream of everlasting life!

If I thirst, let me thirst for His Word. I trust God, and I'm confident that His ways are better than my ways. His will is better than my own choices or preferences. His power and strength will carry me through my times of weakness.

Yesterday, when I was at the hospital, I realized for the first time that I impact the lives of my caregivers (just as much as they impact me). Each one of them: the girl that takes my blood, the receptionist that checks me in, the nurse that takes my vitals, the volunteers, the nurse that removes my port access, my doctor, the girl that schedules my appointments. They cry when I cry. They laugh when I laugh. They pray for me.

I was told several times yesterday that I have the best attitude of all of their cancer patients (bearing fruit in a drought situation). I was so focused on helping other patients and trying to get a handle on my own problems, that I hadn't taken into account my disposition and optimism and faith in front of people who see me frequently. It should be our habit to show others that we have confidence in God regardless of our circumstances.

I'm sad when I'm in pain, but the happiness I feel when I'm

honoring God overshadows that pain like a leafy tree branch protecting me from the scorching sun.

I pray you all bear fruit in the midst of your own personal droughts. Not only is that possible, but it is blessed by God.

My Own Advice

Today was still not a good day for me. I was nauseous, extremely tired, and my hands and feet continue to have nerve pain. Something new happened, and I started getting mouth sores (yet another symptom). They are like blisters that pop up inside my mouth... really? What next? I missed my Godchild's engagement party, and I was really looking forward to it (I just wasn't up for it).

My sister called me from the party and wanted to know what advice I wanted written on a picture frame mat to the happy couple. It didn't even take me a second to come up with the best advice I knew to give.

> *"Put first the Kingdom of God, and everything else will fall into its proper place."*
> — Matthew 6:33

That's the priority, right? God First. Everything else is secondary. I'm a complete idiot, for the record. As I heard my own words come out of my mouth, I realized that I haven't been doing that lately. I've let the cancer come first. I let the pain and suffering come first. I let my treatment come first. I slipped right into a pattern without even realizing it.

Have any of you done this without even realizing it? Is God first place in your life every day? All day long? I'm mad at myself for letting my body take over. God knows my needs. I need to be thinking about God's needs. It's time to follow my own advice. I can't let cancer get in the way again...then it really does win.

If I was face to face with God, I wouldn't want to explain why I let cancer overshadow my relationship with Him. He would look at me and say He had a plan for my good, and my worrying about it showed doubt. He would ask me where my trust went. My faith? Why didn't I believe every promise He made to me to be true? All I had to do was keep my thoughts aligned with God's will. Whether I live one more day or five more years, God decides. Not anything on this earth changes that....not test results, not my body's symptoms, not even the worst disease imaginable. So the one that decides my fate is the one that I will put before all else.

Not Taking Things for Granted

Today was still not a good day for me. I was nauseous. I've always said that the only way to truly appreciate something to the fullest is to have it taken away. Everyday we live, we take things for granted. If you are saying, "Not me, I appreciate everything I have," then let me run a few things by you.

I will be honest and tell you that many of the things I'm going to list were inspired by my 11-year-old son's prayers.

1. <u>We enjoy daylight</u>. In Alaska, they know what it's like to have extended darkness. We are so used to this daily gift that we hardly notice it. What if every day we woke up, we had a black sky?

2. <u>Smells</u>. Simple right? Can you imagine if nothing had an individual fragrance? God could have created things without smells, or everything could smell exactly the same. What purpose does a smell have? If you walked around with a clothespin on your nose all the time, you would really miss fragrances. My favorite smell is fresh bread baking or chocolate chip cookies right out of the oven.

3. <u>Your eyebrows and eyelashes</u>. I took those for granted my entire life, until I got cancer. Don't think you would miss those? Shave your eyebrows off and pluck out every eyelash. I guarantee you would appreciate the time you had them.

4. <u>Taking a shower or bath</u>. Try bathing with a washcloth while standing up without being in a tub or shower for an entire summer and not feeling your whole body submerged in water. You will really miss that refreshing feeling, it's just not the same. Take it away, and you will appreciate

it. I know that feeling after breaking my neck and wearing a harness/halo for a whole summer.

5. <u>Your floors in your house</u>. In some foreign countries, many people live their entire lives in huts with dirt floors. Can you imagine that? Probably not something you think about. Look beneath your feet at home and be grateful for your flooring.

6. <u>Color</u>. Personally, I love this one the most. A life without color? Unthinkable. A black and white world? How depressing that would be!

7. <u>Money</u>. I'm not talking about having less than you desire; I'm talking about having every single cent drained from your bank account. I've had my bank account hit zero after being sick for an extended period. It is the scariest feeling ever to think of losing everything you have worked your entire life to have. Tomorrow, if you woke up and you had absolutely no money, what would that be like? How would you feel? What would you say?

On a more serious note, I try to live each week on this earth as if it were my last. I've had so many people taken away from me. I don't take it for granted that when I'm with someone that I will ever see that person again.

Those that know me, know that I will frequently give out hugs, tell them I love them, express how much I miss them, or appreciate them when I don't see them regularly. That mindset lets you see people differently. What are your parting words when you say goodbye to someone? I know for certain that the last words out of my mouth to my son will be, "I love you more than anything on this earth." I make sure that when I say goodbye to him that those are the last words that come out of my mouth.

Anyway, I could literally write an entire book on the things we should be grateful for. The point is to start looking at things beyond food, shelter, and clothing – the little things we overlook. Be specific when you thank God. He created a tremendous amount and put great thought and detail into the world we live in.

As a child of God, I'm embarrassed by my selfishness of just expecting to have the things I enjoy on a daily basis. You will live a much richer life if your gratitude can grow on a daily basis. We serve an awesome God who has given us more than we deserve. Even when I've lost someone I loved, I had to realize, wow, God put that person in my life for a really long time (it's up to us not to miss the opportunities and to take advantage of that time together building great memories).

All that being said, I am grateful you are here. Every day, in every way, you are treasured. We are all one big family in God's eyes. I pray for your well being and happiness. I pray we can all help each other to appreciate life more through our own personal history of experience.

Share with others things that you are grateful for. Give your friends and family a fresh set of eyes to see the world differently. It will bring you joy too.

Evolution

We can't stop progress; it's been happening for centuries. I thought about my spiritual progression this morning. It took the biggest leap throughout my cancer ordeal and continues to move forward at a rapid rate. Usually, our worst circumstances help us evolve the most spiritually.

Recently, an opponent in volleyball was very rude to me. When I gave her a compliment after the game, she flat out insulted me and then went on to fling one mean comment after another at me over the next two games we played. I was shocked. I couldn't believe my own ears. She's in her 20's and hates to lose to me – an extremely competitive girl (not that I'm one to talk since I'm overly competitive too... we are a lot alike). I later found out from her partner that she was embarrassed by her behavior, but after two weeks went by, I realized she wasn't going to give me the apology I was waiting for. I read in a devotional at the two week mark that when others do us wrong, our first inclination is to hold a grudge and want to get even (which was definitely true in my case). I was angry and hurt.

God, however, had a different plan for me. He helped me think: "What if I was in her position and God were in my position. How would I handle the situation differently?"

I sent her a text that read, "Let's wipe the slate clean...forgive and forget... act like the last time we played each other never happened. We are grown women and both of us are capable of behaving with class and dignity. I love volleyball and want it to be a good experience when I go out on the court without any negativity. Volleyball is my escape from all the hardships I have suffered, and believe me when I say that I've suffered enough. I respect you as a player. What do you say?"

Her response: "I totally agree, and I was really embarrassed by my behavior afterwards. It was a coping mechanism for me."

The old me would have been mad at her and not spoken to her until I got an apology— I would have been waiting forever. The old me would have told everyone what a jerk she was. The old me would have looked for an opportunity to get even. The old me would have carried a grudge and drank it like poison every time I saw her. Yay, that I'm not the old me anymore!

I'm a child of God that has evolved. I've grown spiritually. I've matured. I've learned to look at the world through different eyes. I set a wrong right even if I didn't do it. It felt good inside to extend an olive branch. Sure, I realize she may have continued to be mean to me. It could have ended differently, but that wasn't God's plan. God's plan was for me to do the mature thing spiritually. After all, doesn't He do that with us on a daily basis? He forgives us no matter how many times we wrong Him in some way.

My Prayer

Father God,

Thank You for helping me evolve and progress spiritually. Sometimes I forget that I'm not the same person anymore. It's true that when we enter into a relationship with You that a new life has begun. Help me continue to grow in ways that make You happy. It feels good to be more like You. I gladly say goodbye to the old me and welcome the ever evolving new me. I love You...I love Your ways...I love the path You set before me...Thank You for walking with me.

Amen.

Escaping the Trap

We all do it at some time or another — fall into the trap of others. There's so many of them; how could we possibly avoid it? One of the worst ones for me is meeting someone else's expectation and making myself miserable in the process. Think about that for a moment; it's an ongoing process. You do that your whole life for your parents, teachers, friends, spouse, kids, boss, etc., and the moment you realize you have fallen into that trap and try to break away from that pattern of approval, it is met with resistance and disapproval.

One of the greatest gifts I received during my cancer ordeal was a framed picture from my younger sister that had writing inscribed on beach sand. It read, "Remember Who You Are."

Those are powerful words. I could add to that and say, "Remember Who God Says You Are."

God would NEVER say, "How's my little failure doing today? What's my little loser up to? I can't believe you would attempt something you obviously aren't capable of doing."

NOPE! God would never say that; He would be quite the opposite.

How do we escape the trap of social acceptance and widespread approval of others? We stop looking around us and start looking up. God's approval should be at the top of our to-do list every single day. When I get to heaven, I won't be going over my inventory of clothes and jewelry. I won't be discussing how I kept my yard up. I won't be giving God the keys to my car and saying here, "I worked really hard to get this for you." I won't ask Him if He was impressed by my job. AND, I definitely won't say, "I just followed someone else's lead because I wanted to fit in with the world."

I am who God created me to be. I follow a path that sometimes, when I look around, it's just me – solo. I have priorities that fit into His destiny for me and not what others would do in my shoes. I don't have to justify my decisions, but I do need to commit to them without wavering or letting doubt cloud my judgment.

BE YOU. Everybody else can be them. There is no one quite like you, and that is how God intended you to be — a rare treasure.

My Prayer

Father God,

I want to make Your approval more important than man's approval. Help me listen to others with a filter. I realize my inner voice doesn't always match up with someone else's outer voice. The more time I spend with You, the better I know what's right for me and how I choose to live the time I have left on this earth.

I'm sometimes saddened by others' judgment of me. I don't want to be, but my feelings get hurt when I sense their disapproval or rejection. I have to be honest with You, because there is no way to hide the truth from You. I go back to that short, but to the point, prayer.

After a lifetime of falling into the trap of living a life dictated by social norm, guide my steps to avoid worldly pitfalls. I want to look at You in heaven and say, I tried my best to please You and Your will for my life.

In Your precious son, Jesus' name,

Amen.

Excuses, Excuses

I've never been a big fan of excuses since I have a "get it done no matter what" mentality.

I even made my son get in the car when we were both sick (and it was pouring down rain) to drop off something all the way across town to a friend's house for her party just because I said I would. I was trying to teach my son responsibility and dependability. My job is founded on results and not excuses. I'm extremely hard on myself (and others) because of it.

At what point do I give myself a break?

Cancer took away several years from my life. It's like being robbed and violated at the same time. The ripple effect touched every aspect of my life, and years of neglect creep up on you: my house, my yard, my car, my finances, my personal relationships, my job, my body, my wardrobe, and even my mail. Jumping back into life is not a very easy transition when you are trying to fix everything at once while being a full time mom, having ongoing medical problems and doctor appointments, and going through a divorce simultaneously. Excuses, excuses, right? The stress of it is causing me to have panic attacks with chest pains.

Why am I baring all to tell you this? Because I want you to give yourself a break. It took years to create the neglect; it will take years to get back on track. Whatever you are behind on or goals that aren't yet achieved (from weight loss to emotional well being), take your first step, and then your next, and then your next.

I know life gets overwhelming sometimes, and we make excuses not to move on because of our imposed limitations. At times, it feels like you are just keeping your head above water. If anybody gets that - it's me.

Accept help with Thanksgiving. Pray with Hope. Don't give up. Press Forward. If you are tired, rest. If you are sad, cry. If you are stressed, then relax. If you are behind, take care of what you have control over today.

Whatever your excuses are, I'm sure they are valid, but after you have given yourself permission to not be perfect, make a plan to move on and expect life to hand you delays. Then, formulate a new plan until you find a formula that works for you.

Discouragement over past failures will not serve your future, so say goodbye to yesterday and know that today is a new day. Success is knocking on your front door!

My Prayer

God,

Thank You for giving me not only the tools I need to succeed, but friends and family to help me use them, especially when I get tired or overwhelmed. Help me get over the hump of impatience and disappointment.

I know anything is possible through You. You are a God of justice, restoration, and completeness. I lean on You for these things to be a reality in my life. I trust You with all that I am and all that I can be. Heal not only my physical body but also my surroundings, so that I may know peace.

Amen.

So What Are You Going To Do About It?

My son was saying that he felt sorry for a particular person, and I responded with, "So what are you going to do about it?" I know that caught him off guard.

"What do you mean? What am I going to do about it?"

"Give me some examples of what you can do to make that person's situation better."

That was the easy part. He listed several things he could do to improve her life and offer support and expressions of love.

Then I said, "Those sound great! Let's get started doing those things right away." After we did, he saw just how easy it is to make someone smile and bring them joy because they know someone cares and not only thought of them, but showed them care through their actions.

Why aren't we all doing this every chance we get? I know (because my friends are so great) you will all say, "Are you kidding me? I help people all the time." I would answer you by posing the question, "Do you help people when it's inconvenient for you, especially when you're not that close to them? Are there people around you in need that you literally have the resources to help them, but you haven't had the time? How about complete strangers? Do you show them you are God's child by your words and actions everywhere you find yourself during the day? Grocery stores, gas stations, parking lots, restaurants, the soccer field, doctor's offices...you know, places other than church?

If you look me in the face and tell me that you've done all you can do to help others because your family (or work) takes up the majority of your time; you just don't have the energy;

your plate is full; or whatever excuse you feel like using I will tell you this: God's family is HUGE. If you plan on doing good and reaching out to those who are silently screaming for help, God will carve out the things you need to get that job done... whether it's money, time, confidence, connections, or transportation.

God didn't create us all to barely get by and focus inward on ourselves. He created you to SEE and DO and LOVE. Even if it's something as small as taking ice cold drinks to people who are hot and work outside all day. In their eyes, that's huge. It means you saw them and you care about their comfort.

Last night, someone took my shopping cart back to the store for me. Small gesture? Not for me. I was exhausted, and the pain in my spine was killing me last night. I really appreciated that. I'm thankful for the gift every week of my neighbor bringing in my trash can from the curb. He goes one step further and does the whole block. Get the picture?

Look around (you won't have to look too far) and THINK, "What am I going to do to make that person's life better?" Then, GO DO IT!

If you are already a giving person, stretch yourself and do just one more thing a week a little outside your comfort zone. I promise God will bless you for it, and it will become addicting to multiply joy.

Investing

There are 1,440 minutes in a day. I don't know about you, but I don't want to waste a single one of them. I know I have to sleep and eat which, combined, takes away almost half of those minutes.

The other day, I got stuck on the phone listening to someone prattle on about the most mundane subjects. I really just wanted to interrupt and say, you are wasting some of my precious minutes! I can't afford to lose any more. I've wasted too much time already. When I see a bad movie, I think, "There goes two hours I'll never get back."

Don't waste any of your minutes living someone else's life. Don't waste your minutes worrying about anybody else's opinion of what you do or who you are. Don't waste your minutes in anger, fear, regret, jealousy, or sadness. You've got one life that you get to live... one day at a time.

I have learned the hard way what's important in life. I used to say the best thing that could happen to somebody is a hurricane. It forces you to make choices about what truly matters and honestly, all of a sudden, what doesn't hold a place at all. Looking at the world on the edge of death more than once, for me, I would say, "God is the only thing I need." For when I take my last breath, if I don't have Him, I have nothing that will serve any purpose.

Invest your time, your efforts, your thoughts, your heart and soul wisely, because you never know when the storm is coming. What would you grab from your home if it were on fire? I would already have what I need to survive. The rest is just stuff.

What We Leave Behind

"But godliness with contentment is great gain. For we brought nothing into the world, and we can take nothing out of it."

— 1 Timothy 6:6-7

Now you know where they get the phrase: "You can't take it with you."

Whatever we spend a lifetime accumulating just becomes nothing more than a big pile of stuff. During our lifetime, contentment should be found in our closeness to God instead of the things we buy. Since we can't take anything with us, we should be thinking more about what we leave behind.

What has always drawn me to creating things is that they can be enjoyed by others long after I'm gone: the canvases I paint on, the letters I write, anything that reflects God's inspiration and creation in nature, and things that can be passed down from generation to generation. The relationships that you foster are another perpetual thing to be enjoyed after you leave.

What kind of impact did you make on others? Did anyone get closer to God because of you? Did you teach your children as many life lessons as possible? Did you show appreciation and love people just the way they are? How did you help others through the ways God blessed you? Were you a source of encouragement to those who needed it? How did you use your spiritual gifts to glorify Him?

Only God is the source of true contentment, so what gift will you leave earth in His name?

You Can't Take It With You

I know you probably think I'm going to write about how you can't take money with you when you die, but I'm not. I'm going to talk about letting go of even more important things. I've had time to reflect on my life and upcoming death with regards to how God wants me to plan.

When you enter into the gates of Heaven, these are some of the things that you can't take with you: grudges, anger, resentment, jealousy, hurt, mistakes, regret, retaliation, and sadness (to name a few). Those things don't belong in Heaven. They don't belong because they have no place, they serve no purpose, and they carry no value.

What would happen right now, at this very minute, if you just let go of all the things that have built up over time when others have hurt you? Simply, just let it go because it serves no purpose for your future. You're right...they are wrong... but if you died tomorrow, it really wouldn't matter who is right and who is wrong. Your only concern, then, would be if you were right with God.

Were you in good standing? What if you just forgave everyone? Did you forgive someone for insulting you and hurting your feelings? Did you forgive the person who lied to you and about you? Did you forgive the person that was mean to you? Did you forgive the person that ignored you in your time of need? Did you forgive the person that embarrassed you (on purpose nonetheless)? Did you forgive the person that used you and constantly took from you? Did you forgive the person that gossiped about you? Did you forgive the person that abandoned you? Did you decide to not let that built up anger into your life anymore?

All those people have no influence over your peace of mind.

You could do that, you know. Let it ALL go. All it takes on your part is a decision not to let anyone steal your joy.

Jesus didn't have any sin that He needed to pay for yet, he readily paid for ours. Upon asking, Jesus forgives us in an instant, and that mistake is gone for good – erased. Can we not extend that same gift of forgiveness to others too and get right in the eyes of God?

I've got news for you, if you don't get this today, you will later. All that pent up junk you carry around emotionally will be the weight too heavy to carry into heaven. Don't wait until it's too late. Let me be your warning. Let go, because God will make us reap what we sow. Sow seeds of Goodness. Do it because you have God's goodness within you, and He will help you achieve this goal.

I guarantee you that when you forgive, a peace will wash over you, the likes of which you have never known. It feels so good to let go. You will experience freedom from a heavy, spiritual chain that bound you to that other person.

Don't go another day spending another minute of irritation. Your time and purpose are far too valuable for that. You can't take it with you... so let it go.

Chapter 14

Thanksgiving and Praise

Thanksgiving Blessings

"Know that the Lord, He is God; It is He who has made us, and not we ourselves; We are His people and the sheep of His pasture. Enter into His gates with thanksgiving, And into His courts with praise. Be thankful to Him, and bless His name. For the Lord is good; His mercy is everlasting, And His truth endures to all generations."

— Psalm 100:3-5

I actually wrote several different versions of this all in an effort to at least try to articulate my gratitude, but nothing seemed to come close to expressing the depth of my appreciation for the blessings in my life.

I realized in order to tell you what I am thankful for, it would be best to describe how I got to this place of the deepest gratitude I've ever known.

I know what it's like to be alone. I know what it's like to be so sick that death whispers in your ear. I know what it's like to be flat broke with the fear of losing everything. I know what it's like to be so sleep deprived and overworked, that you get dizzy and your whole body shakes with cold. I know what it's like to be lied to and treated unfairly. I know what it's like to lose several people close to you. I know what it's like to feel trapped in a horrible marriage.

And as sad as all of that may sound, it's not. It's a gift: a great blessing. Because I have known the "without" moments, I can now truly appreciate the "with" moments.

But I am most thankful for the blessing of having a relationship with God; it is a gift I have never been without. The rest is just "stuff."

This Thanksgiving, my blessings rise to new heights because I no longer live in a valley of doubt, fear, pain or discouragement. I have a renewed faith that gains strength daily.

My Prayer

Thank you God for guiding me, encouraging me, and saving me; YOU are my biggest blessing ever. I am whole in Your presence and eternally grateful.

A Thankful Heart

A thankful heart wakes up every morning before getting out of bed and says, "Thank You, Father, for another day on this earth with the ones I love."

A thankful heart sings loudly because its inner joy cannot be contained in such a small space inside the human body; it has to be set free.

A thankful heart gives without hesitation because Jesus gave all of Himself to the thankful heart first.

A thankful heart prays because knowing love means knowing the source of all love.

A thankful heart forgives, because it cannot look backwards and always focuses on the new day.

A thankful heart still trusts, because distrust comes from a place that the thankful heart stays away from. That trust isn't in mankind or worldly ways, but that trust resides in The Lord who holds the thankful heart carefully in the palm of His hand.

A thankful heart wears its gratitude like a beautiful coat for all to see.

A thankful heart goes to bed at night with a smile because it sleeps on a pillow of blessings, and it lets its struggles and trials sleep outside in the cold.

A thankful heart calls out to other thankful hearts, and, in each other's company, they never stop growing.

May you know the uncontainable freedom, joy, and peace that your own heart has. We have everything to be thankful for because we are all God's children. We have the common bond of royal DNA. I cherish being the daughter of the King of Kings. Our family is huge. I love you greatly, because it's the only way God intended me to be.

"Make my joy complete by being like-minded, having the same love, being one in spirit and of one mind."
— Philippians 2:2

Let Love Guide Your Life

"Most of all, let love guide your life, for then the whole church will stay together in perfect harmony. Let the peace of heart which comes from Christ be always present in your hearts and lives, for this is your responsibility and privilege as members of His body. And always be thankful."
— Colossians 3:14-15

Notice that the last line of this verse, is "Always Be Thankful!" True Appreciation for things often comes from having to work for them or waiting patiently for them. Focus on the end result of what you are going to love in the end.

Take note! The happiest people don't necessarily have the best of everything; they just make the most out of what they've been given and everything that comes their way. So, open your eyes to your blessings and the happiness that sprouts from it. Give thanks to God, for His love has impacted your life far beyond what you could think.

First and foremost, I LOVE GOD. Love is a privilege that I don't take for granted. If we would put Love front and center in our lives, there would be little room left for anything else to bring us down.

May you find countless reasons to Love your day and your life!

Thank God for Everything

In my quiet time, before I headed off to Duke for another day of needles and tests, I thanked God for everything. I'm not talking about just the good stuff either. I thanked Him for EVERYTHING. Every accident, every argument, every hurt feeling, every tear, every injustice, every surgery, every needle, every "from bad to worse day," and yes…even for my incurable cancer… ALL OF IT. For the record, I've never done that before. Ever. I never thanked God for every single hurtful thing I've ever endured or have yet to face… and truly mean it.

You know what comes after saying that prayer? Calm. Peace. Understanding.

The greater the suffering, the more you learn what God wants you to know. If I were up in heaven and I had to choose my path before I was even born, I wouldn't pick the easy one. My soul wouldn't benefit from that. If I could see the future and realize how my soul would evolve from horrible circumstances, I know me…I would choose the hard road.

Why? Because I'm…

· More empathetic
· Charitable
· Understanding
· Thoughtful
· Selfless
· Grateful

I'm also closer to God, and I feel like I can really read, understand, and live His word on a deeper level.

Last time I checked, those are all really great things – all from my suffering.

Don't let your tragedies be in vain— learn from them. Let your soul evolve and quit fighting God. I promise that, in the end, what was meant for your harm will be for your good.

I know from the outside looking in, my friends and family feel sorry for me. People pity me. They worry about me. It's hard for them to see me be in pain, and they all dread my death. Yet, I'm more prepared than anyone I know to march forward.

It may not seem like it by my circumstances, but I KNOW GOD IS SMILING when He watches me. He's proud of who I've become. That means more to me than anything else I could ever have or achieve. I just want to be the best soul I can be before I leave this earth. Cancer doesn't stop that from happening...it gives me a new perspective that I couldn't have any other way.

My Prayer

Father,

I know You love me. You show me in countless ways. Even in my darkest hours, You give me light...my family, my friends, my faith, and the unlimited power of prayer. You teach me, because I'm willing to learn.

I don't doubt for one second that I will be a better soul because of the cup of suffering I'm about to drink from. Just be with me every second and constantly remind me that everything has a greater purpose. I will do my best to tell others what You mean to me.

Thank You God for letting me evolve into the daughter that pleases You!

Amen.

Chapter 15

I Am a Source Of...

What Are You a Source Of?

"We can complain because rose bushes have thorns, or rejoice because thorn bushes have roses."

— Abraham Lincoln

I read this morning about God's wrath. Yes... everyone loves the glossy butterfly lovey sunshine version of God, and no one wants to hear about what He does when He's angry. Let's just say a God that created all things can just as easily destroy them in a not so pleasant fashion. This is a God that split the ocean in half as easily as we part our hair. Words like... slaughter, crush, destroy, punish, weeping bitterly, plagues, and terrible distress...make us cringe.

Fortunately for us, God doesn't rule us daily with fear and anger, even though He easily could. If He chose that path for us, we wouldn't have any free will, and we would be forced to be slaves to carry out His will. After reading about His judgment and punishment, I thought to myself, "I would hate to be the source of His anger." That got me thinking, "What AM I the source of?" ...to God...to my family... to my friends?

I want to be the source of encouragement, love, forgiveness, understanding. However, I'm sure for some, I'm the source of frustration, impatience, hypocrisy, and irritation. I know what you're thinking, "Sweet 'lil Teresa... No Way!" Yes way.

I'm overbearing with my opinion sometimes. I have a hard time listening to complainers. I'm not very tolerant of lazy people (even though I'm lazy sometimes and enjoy hanging out in the house in my PJs on some days). I whine about not having a man in my life (Hello??? What's wrong with this picture?). I'm a perfectionist to the point of obsessive compulsiveness (if things aren't exactly straight, or even clean enough, or put together the way I would do it). I take longer to do things (like painting my house) because I think speed equals sloppiness. I think I'm right 80% of the time (20% of people are smarter than me...there are, after all, rocket surgeons out there... please tell me you get that joke... there is no sarcasm font).

My point is this: What I WANT to be the source of doesn't always line up with what I'm ACTUALLY the source of for other people and for God. Wanting something isn't enough. I have to change myself in order to live out that desire for my character. Being honest with yourself isn't easy, and sometimes it can make you feel ashamed.

There are times where you have such a build up of past mistakes that you don't think you can wake up and start from scratch to make changes. After all, other people know your history— are they really going to be able to see you in a new light? My answer would be...maybe not at first...but, eventually. It took years for you to become who you are now. It may take years to become who you really want to be. The important thing is to decide and take the first step toward the direction you want to go in.

What are you the source of to other people... to God?

What do you want to be the source of? What can you do to change the things in yourself that you don't like? How can you amplify the qualities that you love in yourself?

If you would have asked me six years ago what my biggest goal was, I wouldn't have answered to be a source of inspiration and encouragement to others; to make people think about their life choices; to spread the love that God has for me to others so that they may never know a day without that love. I was just going with the flow and reacting to whatever life handed me.

Now, I have answered my wake up call with a life filled with purpose and meaning every day I wake up. I never want to disappoint God. I never want to be at the end of my life and feel that I wasted a single precious day.

There are definitely changes that still need to be made, since I'm trying to match up my wants with my character. Better now than judgment day (I don't think God will give me a longer grace period than a lifetime).

Good Luck with whatever changes are in your future. I know you have it in you to be your best self!

Goals

"What you GET by achieving your goals is not as important as what you BECOME by achieving your goals."
— Henry David Thoreau

In order to prosper and flourish, you have to set some sort of goals for your life. I know everyone thinks about this at New Years as a chore, but without doing so on a regular basis, you are short changing yourself. Indifference equals limitation.

I realize all of that sounds trite and overly generic, so I will break it down for you in my usual "tell it like it is" fashion...

YOU WERE MEANT FOR MORE!

Kudos to you for whatever you have made it past, through, or over. Kudos to you for getting out of bed every morning regardless of what you dread. Kudos to you for all your wonderful trophy, blue ribbon, let's bake her a cake moments!!!! YAY YOU! Now what's next to get you where you want to be as a person...as a Christian? If you are already perfect, by all means, quit reading this immediately.

I truly think it's as simple as a list of adjectives. Describe on a sheet of paper the "you" that you want to be remembered by others (after you are gone), and include the qualities that you want God to see in you when it's time to see Him face to face.

How are we looking? Are we there yet? Room for improvement anywhere? If no changes are needed, go ahead and retire in the tropics and send me some postcards. If there are some goals that still need setting in some area of your life, let's get cracking! You have some benefits waiting impatiently for you right now.

Don't be content with going through the motions every day

– that is an empty life. Don't surround yourself with lazy, uninterested, and shallow people or those who are content with being mediocre. Fire yourself up! Motivation is a prayer away! Show the world what you're capable of!

"Do not put out the Spirit's fire."

— Thessalonians 5:19

Knowing how God sees you and His intentions for your life is like pouring gasoline on your goals; expect your small dreams to ignite into huge dreams, so build your bigger, better bonfire right now! Become the person you envision, and don't limit yourself to being the person everyone else generically stereotypes you to be.

I know for a fact, that you are capable of achieving anything you set your mind to; better yet, God has unlimited capabilities of achieving anything you set your heart and soul to! Set your goals and BE the man or woman that YOU and God both know you can be.

I say all these things out of good intentions to encourage you to be your best and live your best!

Enough

Have you ever just had enough?! Sick of people blatantly lying to you? Excluding you? Taking advantage of you? Putting you at the bottom? Cutting you off in traffic? Doing a poor job and expecting twice the pay? Being surrounded by grouchy, ungrateful, lazy and yes, stupid people? At some point you just want to scream, "Enough! I've had it! Why can't you see how ridiculous you're being? You frustrate me! What's wrong with you?"

It's not likely that you will ever do that in real life, but I'm sure people would be shocked if they could only hear what goes on inside our heads. We are thinking those things and just not saying them out loud. Guess what? People can't hear our thoughts, but God can.

Yikes, I know. It's a sobering thing to think about. I'm not saying that you are going to be able to look at irritating people and think, "As another child of God, I love you no matter what." I don't think that's realistic because of our human nature. What I'm suggesting is to step away from them or the situation and just say HIS NAME because He is the one that has patience, the one that has understanding, the one that can forgive our negative thoughts, and the one that paid the price for our sinful nature.

"JESUS, help me calm down and put my thoughts on your kingdom. Don't let my thoughts sit angrily and fester, not here, not now, and not in this place. Your Father wants me to rejoice in the life He has planned for me. Don't let that person steal my joy. Your love and grace is ENOUGH to help me when I say your name. Jesus, help me walk away in peace and leave my negative thoughts behind."

I dare you to try it; it actually helps. I've put it into practice.

Jesus can do what you can't. Strength is my word for the year. Learning this coping skill has strengthened me, because I could actually stew for hours and days when people would wrong me in some way. Now, I have regained control over my thoughts by practicing this. I've strengthened my happiness. To coin a phrase: "It's a good thing!"

Complain Free Challenge

I have an interesting fact for you this morning...the Bible contains approximately 7,500 promises in it. Impressive, don't you think? Guess what ISN'T mentioned anywhere near that? Complaints.

When you describe Jesus, you never say, "Jesus was really quite the complainer. People were just naturally drawn to His complaining nature. Jesus was the perfect complaining role model." RIDICULOUS! I can only imagine how offended God must be when He hears us complain. The minute we spout off yet another complaint about a person or situation, He must think, "Have they learned nothing?" The sad part is, we do it more often than we even realize out of sheer habit.

Feel free to stop reading this part if you never complain.

We complain about our weight, our hair, our age, our health, our finances, our exes, our family, people we know, our government, violence, education systems, people we hire and fire, the world at large, and yes, quite shockingly, we complain about people we love.

I'm sure you can add to that list. Think about this past week. How many times did you have conversations that included complaining? I will be the first to step up and say, I'm guilty of complaining. The worst part is: Complaining only accomplishes three things:

1. You have to relive the problem by telling it, and that honestly doesn't make you feel any better about it.

2. You drag in whoever is listening to you, and that certainly isn't an attractive quality that

would make them like you more. (Probably why Jesus isn't remembered for being a complainer).

3. You offend God. (Need I say more?).

To clarify, I am so disappointed in MYSELF that I want to make a change. So, I intend to challenge myself to "complaint-free" days. For the next three days, I will honestly do my absolute best not to complain about anything. Not traffic. Not the price of something. Not inferior craftsmanship. Not my aching back. Not house repairs... I mean, Nothing!

Will it be hard? Unfortunately, yes. How sad is that? Every time I am tempted to complain, I'm going to say I love_____ (blank) instead. I challenge you to be more accountable too. If not for yourself then to honor your Father.

If you are up for the challenge, Good Luck and let your friends help you.

God Is Not Finished Yet

"Be confident of this, that he who began a good work in you will carry it on to completion until the day of Christ Jesus."
— Philippians 1:6

I tried my three day no complaint challenge, and I failed. I tried sticking to a diet and workout routine, and I failed. I tried to get ahead on my projects and meet all my deadlines, and I failed. I tried to find the best in some "hard to love" people, and I failed. I tried to maintain my patience but found my irritation just grew. My point in telling you about my failures is this...

Just because you want something and put forth effort towards that goal, it doesn't make it so.

Fortunately, for all of us...God doesn't look at our failures and say, "You only get one chance, and since you totally blew it, I'm not going to invest any more time with you." It's quite the opposite actually.

God's influence on us is a lifelong process. Yesterday, today, and tomorrow, He will continue to help us evolve into being better children of God. I can't imagine living a life without His promises.

God isn't finished with me yet; I continue to be a work in progress, but I will not give up because I have a Father who has taught me not to be a quitter!

May our failures merely be our first attempts in a long line of future success stories.

A Prayer for Forgiveness
and Peace of Mind

God,

Please forgive me for all my imperfections and for all the wrong I have done.

Give me the grace to forgive those that have hurt me.

Amen

A Prayer for Forgiveness of
Those Who Have Hurt Me

Dear God,

Please forgive those that have hurt me because I forgive them.

Amen

"What a wonderful God we have – He is the Father of our Lord Jesus Christ, the source of every mercy, and the one who so wonderfully comforts and strengthens us in our hardships and trials. And why does He do this? So that when others are troubled, needing our sympathy and encouragement, we can pass onto them this same help and comfort God has given us. You can be sure that the more we undergo suffering for Christ, the more He will shower us with His comfort and encouragement."

— 2 Corinthians 1:3-5

Chapter 16

Heart After God's

Respect

"So the last will be first, and the first last. For many are called, but few chosen."
— Matthew 20:16

I have learned that the best way to have people listen to you is to earn their respect. Keep in mind that this process can be very slow. Actions always speak louder than words, so it is vital to show others who you are by your actions and the results that you have achieved through those actions. You may be wondering...why am I even making this point?

I want others to know God and the truth about their own salvation. If I shared that information with those who don't know me well, they would HEAR me but not really LISTEN with their hearts. After you build relationships with love, trust, and respect as your foundation, people will listen to you, and I mean really listen to what you have to say.

It can take years for friends or family members to finally

185

approach you and question why you are so different from anyone else they know. Now is the time to SHOW the world that you are God's child with your behavior. Live your life enriched, and lead by example. Earn the respect of those around you. Eventually, they will come to you with a listening heart because of the groundwork you have built.

To gain respect, you must first respect others. Even if you don't agree with their views on religion, politics, money, or morals, you can respect them as a person, as another Child of God. Their life choices might not line up with yours at all, but you can love them the way Jesus loves you. They will admire that quality in you that sets you apart. You will be a light so bright that it would be hard to ignore you. Then, pick your moment to speak about your perspective on living a fulfilled life. They will listen to you out of respect first and understanding second.

Don't give up on those that seem too far gone, stubborn, complacent, or lost. They need you the most. If not you, then who will step in and care about them? Where will they find the answers they so desperately need? What they have turned to in the past isn't working in their life, every bandaid...every distraction...every bad habit...has piled up so high that they need someone to dig them out. That angel on earth could be you. Start with respect and God will lead you to what's next.

"Always be prepared to give an answer to everyone who asks you to give the reason for the hope that you have. But do this with gentleness and respect."

— 1 Peter 3:15

Your Greatness

God determines your greatness by how many people you serve, not how many people serve you.

I've had several conversations with my mom about who has been helping me through the worst year of my life. The family members, friends, and neighbors who have given their time, resources, and love are truly the greatest people I've ever known.

God doesn't need to hear about their deeds from the people they tell. God sees who they are when no one else knows.

I spend many nights crying alone in my room when I think about what I've lost through this cancer. I think about the loved ones I'm leaving behind. I think about the freedom I once had that has been ripped away. I've never been so broken. I have been humbled beyond words.

My relationships are the only thing I have left. It's all I have that's important to me. Nothing else really matters. My relationship with God is at the top of my list. I know my life served His purpose. I did my best to always do the right thing, to serve others, to be a good friend, sister, daughter, and mother. Here I am, hanging on by a thread. What would I do without those who are strengthening that thread with their Christian service to me through prayer and good deeds?

This is for you.

You who are GREAT according to The Lord. You who unselfishly serve others. You who are created in God's own image... which is Great. You who are treasured, appreciated, and loved. Your Father, who created you, says, "Your care for others is the measure of Your Greatness."

Thank you for sharing Your Greatness with me. I pray for you to be repaid by God tenfold and to enjoy an eternity of reward in Heaven.

Pieces of Light

There is no sugar coating it. Cancer is awful.

It has contaminated my body and has just been eating me up from the inside out. Unfortunately, my outside now looks like my inside: very, very sick. I'm pale, overweight, bald, with no eyelashes or eyebrows. Frankly, I'm too tired and weak to cover it up with makeup, wigs, and outfits. I'm really too sick to even care about my outside appearance anymore. It's depressing to look in the mirror at the 90 year old man staring back at me. The pain in my bones feels unbearable at times. When will this suffering end?

In my dark mood, I think, "How will I move past this?" How does anyone move past depression and a reality they don't want to face? The answer is – you look for pieces of light. Light comes in many forms: *A hug is light. A smile is light. Laughter is light. Loved ones are light. Above all, God is light.*

You hang on to those pieces of joy wherever and whenever you can get them. Some days are better, and some days are worse.

I'm not the old me anymore and honestly, I'm not too thrilled with the new me. So, I will continue to move forward by letting go of both notions and ask God to reach down from heaven and give me pieces of light each day until I am filled up with nothing but light.

Thank you to every single person who has said a prayer for me. I'm grateful for those pieces of light. I'm not done fighting by a long shot; I've just had the wind knocked out me.

The Lord said, "LET THERE BE LIGHT," and there was light. I'm looking forward to the day that the dark corners of my life will no longer be able to hide from the light that a GOD has in store for me.

Waiting for Your Turn

When you were a kid on the playground, your parents would caution you to wait your turn. Didn't it feel like that waiting period was at least a week for you to get on those swings or slide down that slide? Some kid was always in front of you taking FOREVER with his turn, or another kid would cut in line. Hey! He didn't wait his turn!

As an adult, you may be wondering, "When is God going to let me have my turn? Isn't He watching all of us? That person is getting their turn way too long, and that other person clearly cut in front of me. I'm not even sure that the other person deserves a turn! Their behavior is horrible!"

As silly as those comparisons sound, it's kind of true isn't it? You may not say it out loud, but you're thinking it occasionally. Some people seem to get all the good breaks. Some really great people have bad things happen to them that they flat out don't deserve. From the outside looking in, that's how it appears.

I'm going to give you a slice of hope today while you're waiting. I read yesterday that Bamboo in China takes five years to get established. Above the surface, you see little to no growth for the first five years. Its root systems underground are growing strong, deep, and widespread. It's a root system so vast that it's nearly impossible to destroy once it takes off. After those five years are up, the bamboo can shoot up as high as 80 feet in less than a year.

That is what God is doing with you while you are "waiting for your turn." You can't see progress above the surface, but underneath God is developing a massive root system within you so you are prepared for the unbelievable growth that happens swiftly when it's your turn. You will be propelled into great favor. Answers to your prayers will be unleashed on a massive scale. Goodness will literally overtake you, and nothing will be able to destroy it.

Wait patiently. Grow your roots. Keep praying. Do the right things. Trust in God. And above all, prepare yourself, because your turn is coming!

God frequently gives us examples in nature for a reason. He could have given every plant the same growth cycles, but He didn't. He didn't create everything the same to show us...to teach us...that we all grow at different rates. I don't know about you, but I checked my calendar. This is my year coming up! My Five Years of hardship are coming to a close. Mark my words...

"Nothing stands in the way of ALMIGHTY GOD'S BLESSINGS when it's your turn." That alone should make you very excited about waiting your turn.

Turn Towards Him

There Is Goodness

"He came to His own, and His own did not receive Him. But as many as received Him, to them He gave the right to become children of God, to those who believe in His name: who were born, not of blood, nor of the will of the flesh, nor of the will of man, but of God."

— John 1:11-13

I have to say that I am deeply humbled by the goodness I have found lately. There are still good people left in the world, and they literally come from all walks of life. It pains me to know that most people feel judged by others. I've seen it happen repeatedly. Those who know me, know that I'm super non-judgmental, and that's why my group of friends is so eclectic. It doesn't really matter to me where you've been or even what you believe...I accept you right where you are. Jesus calls us to love and to be loved (sounds like a Coke commercial, but wouldn't it be nice?).

I've seen that love firsthand just pour out of people. When you have a terminal illness, even the doctors tell you that you will find out who your real friends are. I will go one step further and say that you will find out what people are made of. You find out what motivates people to get out of bed everyday – who is self serving, and who is other serving. People let their true colors show during adversity.

I wouldn't possibly be able to list all the good deeds and kindnesses that others have shown me during this dark time in my life. Let's just say it's enough to let the light come flooding in. There are not enough words to say thank you. I feel like I've written the word Appreciate, Grateful, Thankful, Thoughtful, and Sweet of you at least a thousand times already in my thank you notes, and the words aren't enough. We need bigger words.

My son says I am his everything. I think that sums it up beautifully. God is my everything. My family is my everything. My friends are my everything.

My Prayer

> *God, You are the bomb diggity. I've seen heart after heart feel the need to express the goodness inside of them. I am blown away by the kindness You've brought my way.*
>
> *I know that there are terrible things happening every day, and there are some flat out evil people that do things that horrify us. I pray that those who walk on dark paths get shown a better way; a happier way. In the Bible, You say that Your care for others is the measure of Your greatness. I am surrounded by greatness. Thank You for that enormous gift in the midst of my suffering. It makes my time on earth better...and I hope it gives You hope the way it gives me hope. May the goodness in us all rise above the sadness, anger, and jealousy that keep us away from knowing the mercy of what Love is capable of.*
>
> *Amen.*

Today, I Speak of Angels

I'm always talking about God and our Lord Jesus Christ, but today, I want to tell you about angels.

When I was a little girl, crying in my bed, I had an angel visit me. I was very upset about my parents fighting, and I knew a divorce was imminent. Despite the turbulence of emotions, I felt a presence sit down beside me (as if it were a real person) placing a hand on mine, gently comforting me. A faint whisper told me that everything was going to be ok: sitting with me until I fell asleep, constantly reassuring me that I was not alone, and washing me in a peace like I've never known. In that moment, I could no longer cry.

That was my first introduction to God. I learned that He is real and is not some far away being that I read about in books.

Angels are all around us. Around the clock, they are protecting us, comforting us, and keeping a watchful eye. They are blessed ministering spirits that accompany us wherever we go. They take care of your loved ones when you aren't with them. I often pray that God would let them stand guard around my home when I sleep at night.

I hope each of you remember that you do have a guardian angel, and they are real. Take comfort in knowing that they are your constant companion on this earth. Thinking of that makes me smile.

There is so much we can't see with our eyes... close them, and you will be surprised how much God will show you.

I Know Who(se) I Am

I was watching a movie last night, and a flirtatious man asked a married woman why he couldn't come inside her house.

Her response to his temptation was, "No... Because I know who I am. I'm married."

I loved that response. It takes guts to say no when you want something. How many times have you been tempted by others to do the wrong thing? Wouldn't the perfect response to any tempter be, "No.... Because I know who I am. I am a child of the Most High God."

Even if you don't say it out loud, that should be the thought that runs through your head. Hanging with the wrong crowd... having one drink too many... flirting when you're married (or they're married)... gossiping about others... little white lies (I believe no lie is little for the record)... Basically ANYTHING that makes you step off God's path.

Know who you are. You are precious and beautiful and created in God's own image. Remember that fact when you interact with others. You belong to a royal family. Hold yourself to a higher standard than those content with far less than God's Best. People will respect you for it, and God will be greatly pleased when you honor Him by maintaining your morals. He's reserved a special place for you in his Kingdom. This place is temporary.

I KNOW WHO I AM. I know my destiny. I know God's expectations of me. I know my choices today affect my life tomorrow. I know that I'm constantly thought of, loved, forgiven, protected, and provided for by God. No person on this earth can make those claims. Why would I ever want to give into their selfish whims when I could be living out my God given intended purpose? I pray you will gain personal strength through your own conviction.

Ask yourself, "Who am I?" And answer by living your life accordingly.

Peace Within Yourself

A long time ago, someone once told me that we are like cars that can't be traded in. We have to take care of ourselves to keep running and make sure that all the parts are in working order. When our own cars break down, we immediately take them in to get repaired, but when something within ourselves isn't working right, we keep taking ourselves out of the garage knowing full well that we could break down on the side of the road at any given time.

Many of us walk around daily not at peace within ourselves.

Ask yourself the following questions:

1. Do you love yourself?...just the way you are right now?

2. Do other people frequently bother you? (yes, that indicates your own level of peace within yourself).

3. Are you troubled by your own shortcomings and weaknesses?

4. Do you wish your circumstances were different?

5. Do you wish you were different?

6. Are you jealous that other people have it easier than you?

7. Are you content? Fully satisfied?

Your answers to those questions should be your eye opener to the level of peace you have within yourself. I may not have your solution to every issue, but I do know the following to be true:

1. Ourselves: You are who God created you to be, and He is not surprised by your strengths or weaknesses. God delights in your self acceptance. Invest your time in things you are gifted in...it helps, not only with your self confidence, but you will gain fulfillment from serving your purpose on this earth.

2. Others: We are all different for a reason (don't expect people to be like you, because you will constantly be disappointed)...we were made to need each other and to learn from each other. If you magnify what you like about someone else instead of harping about what you hate about them, it will change the peace within yourself. If we could learn to be in unity with one another, it would weaken Satan beyond belief.

3. God's teaching lesson: The way we behave under pressure proves to God whether or not we are ready to move on to the next spiritual level. Being at peace with who you are (no matter your circumstances), and being at peace with others (no matter how different they are from us) shows God your spiritual maturity. Our level of inner peace reveals to God and to ourselves what we still need to work on.

You should crave and pursue peace like you do the air you breathe on a daily basis. I've been taking my car in to get worked on a lot recently...mostly maintenance issues. It made me think of my own maintenance issues. Now more than ever, I want inner peace. I realize that all these things are easier said than done. I've got some stuff to work on for sure. The outcome of inner peace is definitely worth the work!

I pray you all find ways to develop your own inner peace more and more each day. It's the best gift you can give yourself.... and God certainly wants you to have it!

Chapter 18

To God Be the Glory

Thank You, Dad

"Now to the King eternal, immortal, invisible, to God who alone is wise, be honor and glory forever and ever. Amen."
— 1 Timothy 1:17

The other night, I was praying, and I started my prayer with the word "Dad." It came out naturally and without hesitation: Dad. It sounds so different, doesn't it? Dad versus Father. You couldn't imagine saying, "Our Dad who art in heaven..." When we pray, it's important that we recognize who God is rather than focus on asking Him for what we want in our prayers. I feel so close to God that sometimes I refer to Him as Dad out of familiarity and closeness (definitely not out of any disrespect).

Anyway, I just wanted to thank Dad for taking care of my needs, for holding my hand through the rough patches, and for being present in my everyday life on a constant basis. My Dad is the greatest! The absolute greatest! I just found out that my cancer is stable with no new growths. My spine, my head, my internal organs, and chest are exactly the same as they were three months ago even though I missed five weeks of chemo because of low blood counts.

That is amazing considering that I have such an extreme progressive and aggressive disease. Dad put His hand on me, and the cancer stood still. When you prayed to Him on my behalf, my Dad's heart was touched, and He covered me in His mercy. My Dad loves me. He loves you too.

Thank you, Dad. I'm so blessed to be Your child.

To God Be the Glory

Sixteen years ago, I found my dream property: two beautiful acres overlooking a large horse pasture. It had over 50 hardwood trees on the front half alone. I spent several years designing the perfect house for that lot with a large circular driveway, gazebo, and a bridge. I envisioned sitting with my toddler son on the front porch and eating homemade chocolate chip cookies while watching the horses romp. It would be fall, and the steps would be covered with pumpkins. The trees would sway in the breeze as their leaves fell to the ground. I'm quite the dreamer — always have been.

Little did I know that my dream wouldn't come to pass. My marriage didn't work out, and I had to fight to get the property in a divorce settlement which became a six year process. My spouse had tried to sell the lot through different realtors during that time and the timing was definitely off. There was no interest whatsoever, even though it was being promoted in several different ways. One day, I got this overwhelming feeling from God that it wouldn't sell until it was all mine. I put it on the market "for sale by owner" two weeks ago. No MLS book. No marketing. No pictures or brochures. I didn't even tell my friends. I thought if God wants it sold, it will happen. He will lead somebody right to it.

Lo and behold, I got a few inquiries early on, and it sold close to asking price within two weeks even though other lots the same size sold for far less over much longer time periods. I stood my ground with my price, because I knew God would make it happen, and He did!!!! I toasted God at dinner for his blessing in our lives. The timing is perfect, because I, quite frankly, need the money. It's such a huge stress taken off of me. My medical bills are through the roof, and I have many expenses as a single mom who can't work. I love God so much.

His timing. His way. His provision. I didn't know 16 years ago what God had planned. Sometimes, it takes awhile for us to get it. It's our job just to trust with 100% Faith. I had so many people telling me what to do, and how to do it. I just kept saying, "God will make it happen. I just know it." My son said, "Maybe this will show others a miracle they can't deny. Maybe it will give them a baby step of faith." I love that my son got to witness what Faith does firsthand. Just a week ago, I told him that I don't know how, but I knew God will provide for us. He always has, and He always will.

To God be the Glory on the sale of my lot. His provision was all over it. It's amazing when you see His power and swiftness when the time is right, firsthand. Some will say luck....others will say it must be the upswing in the economy, and my favorite: just a coincidence. I say GOD. I say prayers answered. I say His plan came to pass. I say Faith trumps circumstances. To God be the Glory.

May you recognize in your own lives that when "your dreams" don't come to pass...the bigger picture may be provision when you need it the most. I will take money to stay alive and to be in my son's life over chocolate chip cookies, fall pumpkins, and horses any day!

From Paralyzed to Energized

I tend to shut down when I'm really suffering. I get quiet. Even on the volleyball court, my partners knew if I wasn't yelling "go" or "move it" or "get there" or "you got it"... something was wrong with me. I felt like I didn't exist this weekend. I didn't return texts or phone calls. I laid in bed in massive pain, crying. When will this stop? How much worse is it going to get? I got invitations to the movies (one I really wanted to see) and the beach....yet I stayed home. Pain can be very crippling.

At 1:00 am last night a couple of sermons came on TV, and I watched... hoping God would speak to me. He did. They were about the enemy. If you are being constantly attacked, it's because Satan is worried about you. He's worried about what you're capable of, and how you can influence others into believing and building stronger faiths. You're on the right track, if you are on Satan's radar. So what does God do to help you in those situations??? He gave David a slingshot against a giant, and I think we know who won that battle! Every harm that the enemy means to use to destroy you, God will deliver you from. In other words, God enjoys throwing it back in Satan's face. God will use my cancer for something very very good. God will use my pain and suffering for something very very good.

I distinctly remember the words, "You will never play volleyball again" from my doctor at the hospital after I broke my neck. He crushed me with those words. I was deflated. I was uninterested in rehab at that point...why bother if I can't do something I love? Then, my spirit got mad! How dare you tell me that when you have no idea what God's plan is for me! I'm going to play, and God is going to help me. I didn't lose a single tournament for two years in a row when I started playing again. I couldn't even turn my neck all the way to the right or left, and I would touch balls beside me and past me based on a feeling and not on sight. It was like God gave me an extra perceptional gift! It was the best season I ever had.

It's important not to be lazy though and lay in bed waiting for God to step in. You have to rise up in belief. You have to declare God's Power over your circumstances. You have to tell your heart, body, mind, and soul every day, "He's coming.... He will show up!" I used to love it when my old business partner would try to wrangle vendors before I showed up on our event installations. She would tell them where things went or what needed to be done next, and occasionally some would fall short...not do their jobs and refuse to do the right thing. Instead of getting mad or fighting, she would look them right in the eye and say, "You haven't seen bad, but it's coming." Meaning....Teresa is on the way, and nothing short of perfection will be tolerated by her...no excuses! That's how I feel about God. I want my pain, cancer, obstacles, and lost time to take note: "God is coming, and you don't want to mess with Him!" That, I can be confident in.

This morning, I woke up feeling well rested. I didn't feel pain for the first time in months. I was, dare I say, COMFORTABLE? It's always a sign for me from God that things immediately improve when I get something through my thick skull that He wants me to hear. I get it. Cancer and Pain meant to harm me ....God will take the Bad and turn it into something Great. Just wait and see. I know it. I believe. My cancer, pain, and suffering will not be in vain...it will somehow lead others to God....it will save many souls.

> *"You intended to harm me, but God intended it for good to accomplish what is now being done, the saving of many lives."*
> — Genesis 50:20

Bless the Name of God

"I bless the Holy Name of God with all my heart. Yes, I will bless The Lord and not forget the glorious things he does for me. He forgives all my sins. He heals me. He ransoms me from Hell. He surrounds me with loving kindness and tender mercies. He fills my life with good things! My youth is renewed like the eagle's!"

— Psalm 103:1-5

It is with extreme gratitude that I give God all the glory for giving me hope this month. You never realize how important hope is until it is taken away from you. Repeatedly I heard the words:

"We can't fix this. We can't heal you. You are terminally ill. Your cancer will never be fully gone from your body. Get your affairs in order. Don't get your hopes up. I'm so sorry. There's nothing more we can do. You have just months to live."

Who wants to be emotionally punched repeatedly without a break? Negative thoughts parading in your head for countless, sleepless, painful nights? Not this girl!

Last night I kept hearing the word, "shelter" whispered in my thoughts. In the midst of my personal storm, God is my shelter. My protector. My provider. My healer. MY HOPE.

God lined everything up before I even knew cancer was trying to take over my entire body. The medicine I'm taking that is doing miraculous things (over 15 years in clinical trials), and friends who bring me food, take me to Duke, run errands, support me and love me. God specifically pointed them out to me one at a time, hand selected. All of my "misfortunes" that I suffered before now?... Merely preparing me for this great battle. A long time ago I remember hearing a gracious speech from someone who had lost, and they said, "It's just not my turn right now. Not my time." That's how I've felt for a very long time. I leave it up to God to decide when it's my turn. He created me. He gets to decide. Hope is me getting a turn. Thank You, God, for Your loving kindness and tender mercies. I will forever Bless Your name!

My Prayer

Father,

The weary world I live in tries to rob me of the joy You want me to embrace every day. There's a constant barrage of negativity meant to bring me down and make me give up. Help me to hear Your whisper of shelter over their repeated shouting.

I bless Your Holy Name. You are the King of Kings. There is no higher power than Yours. You have authority over all in creation.

I will never ever ever forget Your loving kindness when my whole life has been turned upside down, inside out, and crushed beneath the weight of bad news. You rescue me from the depths of sadness and insecurity.

Help me see my soul and not my reflection in the mirror. For my soul is brighter than any star in the night sky. My soul is on fire with a very part of Your own heart Father. I love you eternally.

Amen.

Private Encounters

Throughout the Bible, God spoke to people in private. When we cry out, (alone with our heart's desires) that is when God speaks to us. Allow yourself that privacy. Even the strongest Christians get distracted and overwhelmed— causing them to not prioritize their time with God correctly. You will never go wrong putting God first. You will never regret praying for His will above your own.

One of the biggest prayer mistakes we make is to direct God with our words. Trust me when I say, "He 'gets it' long before you get it." Trust that He loves you more than you love yourself. When you pray for His will, you are letting that love flood into your life.

Do you think it's a coincidence that I started improving when I changed the way I prayed? I don't. As soon as I used my free will to choose His will above my own wants and needs, everything started to get better in my life. Everything started falling into place without my own effort. It's kind of like I was in a boat paddling like crazy against a strong current... and the minute I let go of the paddles, God just let me drift in the right direction.

I quit praying to be healed. I quit praying for help. I quit praying for the pain to go away. I quit praying for my finances. I quit absorbing all the negativity that others lived by. I prayed prayers of gratitude, prayers of God's will above my own, prayers of how I can serve You with the time I have left. Yes...it's that easy.

As humans, we tend to overcomplicate things when it comes to our relationship with God. How many people give you a manual on how to interact with them and know them better? ...and we still don't listen!

I hope my personal experience helps you to let go of your own boat paddles. You don't need to struggle. You don't need to fight for what you want all the time. Let God fight your battles. Just drift. Look at the scenery. Thank God for the scenery and the fact your boat doesn't have a leak. Ask God what He would like for you to do with all that carefree time He has gifted you (when you let Him take over). Notice I said, "Let Him." God always can....but He won't if you don't invite Him in. Like a parent, He will let you learn from your own mistakes.

Do yourself a favor, and find the time and the place to be alone with God. It will change the course of your entire life for the better. Then you will experience Heaven on Earth.

My Prayer

Dad,

I just want to thank You for saving me when I was drowning without help in sight. You changed everything. I was getting really weak and told You I was at the edge of my breaking point. In my weakness, You gave me your strength. You fixed things that I thought were unfixable. You even changed the hearts of some to benefit me in ways I couldn't even think to ask for. You reversed the effects of cancer. Only You can do that. I will never be able to thank you enough for supplying my son's future needs and granting me a break from pain.

I want to extend the mercy You have extended to me. Although I am not perfect, I will constantly strive to give to others and love them the way You love me. I'm so glad You are on the throne! Your will. Your will. Your will. I pray for Your will in my life. In Jesus' name.

Amen.

A Prayer for Reliance on God in the Face of Trials

Thank You God for taking the worst thing imaginable and making it better. I realize that people would rather place blame than make the most of what You've given them. Loud and clear, I say, "NOT ME GOD!" I can and I will find ways to make this situation better...even if it's just enjoying the simple or mundane things in life.

Lord, this life is not my own, it was a gift from You, and I thank You for it. On days when I have strength, I will help others make their life better. I love You for making everything You touch BETTER. I've never looked forward to "better" more than I do right now.

Epilogue

What's Left of My Life
(Teresa's final entry)

"No eye has seen, no ear has heard, and no mind has imagined what God has prepared for those who love Him."
— 1 Corinthians 2:9

Yesterday, I struggled just to stand or walk and had to use a wheelchair at Duke. My heart pumped through my chest, and I could barely breathe if I exerted myself in any way. I just spent the last two months largely alone and rotting away in bed. Even then, I thought God has not forgotten me. God sees me. God has a plan. I still think that's all true, but my wish is not God's will.

Next week, I have to change my son's life forever by telling him that I most likely won't make it to Christmas. Even if I'm alive, it's not the life anybody would want....draining blood from my lungs and getting eaten up from the inside out with cancer. In my heart of hearts, I thought I would go to Duke and my doctor would tell me how to get through this rough patch...this stage of my cancer...this latest challenge. That's been my life for the last two years. Suffer and overcome because God is with me.

With tears in his eyes and a heavy heart, my doctor said

he didn't want to put me through anything else that was unnecessary ....no radiation follow up (big mistake by me that ruined the quality of my life) etc....because I only have a little time left. Now, we will just be reacting to however my body will shut down over the next month. I could have a blood on the brain that could take me immediately (I'm already having vision and headache problems). I could last as long as two months. Chances are, I won't ever be able to climb steps again without enormous pain. I will be going back to Duke tomorrow to get scans done so my doctor is ready for the largest areas of concern. I don't know how I'm going to get through that day. Right now, I have tennis ball sized knots that I thought were nerve endings...it turns out the lymph node cancer has taken over and spread quickly.

With so little time left, how do I spend each day? I want to try to be comfortable. I want closure with all my friends and family. I hadn't even started writing my goodbye letters, because I thought I had more time. Just know that if I don't get to see your face before my funeral comes, I want you to know that I LOVE YOU very much. I have nothing but good memories in my head with you. You have always been a breath of fresh air in my life. You made my life on this earth so much better. No gesture on your part went unnoticed by me. I'm always going to wish I had one more day with you.

God is planning on my immortal life today. My house must be close to ready in heaven. I hope there is never a moment of anger that I'm being plucked from this earth because, as a Christian, isn't this our ultimate goal? For God to take you in His merciful arms and carry you away from earthly pain and suffering?

I love you....eternally and unconditionally....I love you forever.

A Prayer of Thanks

Thank You for all the blessings You have bestowed upon me, my God.

The blessing of a soul, that speck of Your light;

The blessing of the gift of my guardian angel for eternity, who never leaves me even for one second;

The blessing of the peace and love that dwells in me;

The blessing of the family You have given me;

The blessing of those You send into my life for companionship;

The blessing of living in harmony with those around me;

The blessing of my labor, my work;

The blessing of all the material things I have in my life, big and small;

The blessings of this wonderful world and the nature around me.

Thank You, my God for all the things I forget to thank You for. And most of all, thank You God, for continuing to bless my life.

Amen

Thoughts to Leave You With

- If you want to receive love, you have to first give love unconditionally.
- Listen to quality music every day. This is nourishment for the soul.
- Smile and laugh more often (If someone doesn't have a smile, give them one of yours!)
- Live with the three E's: Energy, Enthusiasm, and Empathy
- Life is too short to waste time hating someone.
- Make peace with your past so as not to ruin your present. Everyday, try to live in the moment, and don't dwell on the past.
- It is not necessary to win every argument. One must accept that the other person is not in agreement, and learn from his position.
- Nobody is responsible for your happiness, except yourself.
- Ask yourself everyday, "What three things I am happy about today?"
- Treat others the way you want to be treated.
- Every morning one must say, "My Goal Today is _____." Every night one must say, "I am thankful for_____," and "Today, I succeeded in _____."

- Give others compliments freely and sincerely. It makes you both feel good.

- You can overcome any obstacles — where there is a will there is most definitely a way.

- Do not let an opportunity pass to hug a friend and stay connected with them.

- Don't take yourself so seriously— nobody else does.

- Try to make at least three people laugh everyday.

- Learn something new everyday.

- Whether a situation is good or bad, it will change.

- Remember, we have no control over what others think of us or what happens to us... but only what we choose to do.

- When you help someone else, you heal your own wound.

In God's Love,

Teresa

Teresa's Art

Teresa graduated from the University of North Carolina at Wilmington with a B.A. degree in Fine Arts. This book features her original artworks.

Teresa's art may be found online through Fine Art America and is available there for purchase.

You can purchase Teresa's art by visiting https://fineartamerica.com/art/teresa+koska

or by scanning the QR code below: